Anthony J. Gittins (ed.)
Life and Death Matters. The Practice of Inculturation in Africa

STUDIA
INSTITUTI MISSIOLOGICI SOCIETATIS VERBI DIVINI
Nr. 72

Anthony J. Gittins (ed.)

LIFE AND DEATH
MATTERS

The Practice of Inculturation
in Africa

2000

Steyler Verlag, Nettetal

Die Deutsche Bibliothek - CIP-Einheitsaufnahme

Life and death matters : the practice of inculturation in Africa /
Anthony J. Gittins (ed.). - Nettetal : Steyler Verl., 2000
  (Studia Instituti Missiologici Societatis Verbi Divini ; Nr. 72)
  ISBN 3-8050-0443-5

© Steyler Verlag
Bahnhofstraße 9
41334 Nettetal
Germany

Distributor in the United States:
Anthony J. Gittins, CSSp
Catholic Theological Union
5401 S. Cornell Avenue
Chicago, IL 60615-5698, USA
Tel: 773-753-5343
Fax: 773-728-9466
e-mail: tgittins@ctu.edu

ISSN 0562-2816
ISBN 3-8050-0443-5

Desktop publishing: Steyler Missionswissenschaftliches Institut
Printing: Drukkerij Steijl b.v., Steyl (NL)

Dedicated to the memory of

Harold S. Heard, C.S.Sp. (1913-1999)

and to

Joseph B. Jackson, C.S.Sp. (b. 1915)

Friends
Religious and priests
Faithful followers of Jesus
Dedicated bearers of Good News
Missionaries for the people of Africa
Men of passion and compassion
Makers of memories
Mentors

CONTENTS

BETWEEN NOSTALGIA AND OPTIMISM –
THE GROUND OF HOPE

"When the day of Pentecost came, they were all together in one place. Suddenly a sound like the blowing of a violent wind came from heaven and filled the whole house where they were sitting ..." Not only does this passage evoke nostalgic memories of a gathering in West Africa at the end of 1997, but it is an appropriate way to start a book about inculturation. In the first place, inculturation has a great deal to do with re-reading the Scriptures, recontextualizing them, and bringing them into an engagement with our lives in such a way as to reanimate them; in the second place, the story of that Pentecost moment is itself an illustration of how inculturation of the faith changes lives.

The Consultation in Tamale, Ghana, on which this volume is based, brought some twenty missionary anthropologist theologians together to share experiences of inculturation and to show how theory and practice encounter each other. We acknowledged that, if not exactly a Pentecost moment, that meeting marked a watershed in our lives: there would be no going back, only a commitment to continue the pilgrimage. We sensed, together, and with our bishop in our midst, that something was struggling to be born and that we must welcome it and nurture it. We did not create it and we would not control it; but if it was truly of the Spirit then not only would it not die, it would survive its journey beyond that place and into a wider world.

As the hot dry wind blew in Northern Ghana, we were reminded that although the Incarnational model is a powerful tool for inculturation, we also *need* the Pentecost model: the mighty wind of the Spirit makes things *new*, and if transformation is to occur, then Pentecost offers some clue about what may be entailed.

The Spirit of Pentecost transformed the fearful into the faithful: not that their fear evaporated, but their faith was strengthened. So it must be with us: there are things to fear, but we must not lose faith. Fear of the unknown, of change, of diversity, of failure, or of the scale of the challenge: these are legitimate concerns, but vague and not easy to address. There are other – nearer, more immediate, more tangible – fears and concerns, that threaten to delay, derail or even destroy the process of inculturation. Though recent popes have explained and endorsed inculturation, and though it is officially supported, historically proven, and biblically justified, one senses that something is just not right. At the 1998 Synod for Asia, the clash of ecclesiologies and the contrast of leadership styles between, on the one side (literally) the Asian bishops – especially the Japanese, but others too – and on the other side the Roman authorities, was not only palpable but embarrassing.

In the current mood, one must ask: is inculturation possible without dissent or disobedience? Is pastoral ministry possible without confrontation with curial or papal authority? Can African Christians ever really find a home in the Catholic church? Can the church ever get beyond Eurocentrism? Can we have a polycentric church? Can we develop Uniates or Patriarchates? Can we emphasize *indigenization* as much as *contextualization*? Can we move beyond translation models, and look for *something new:* beyond adaptation to genuine creativity under the Holy Spirit's guidance? Can we pray a new church into being? Can we take local realities as authentic starting points for inculturation?

It is easy to be pessimistic: Liberia, Sierra Leone and the Congo have been "Christianized" for well over a century, yet Christianity appeared to have little impact on the combatants of their bloody and self-destructive civil wars. South African "Christianity" supported the horror-story of Apartheid. And Rwanda and Burundi were trumpeted as the most "Christian" of African countries before the genocide. What does all this mean? What *is* "Christianity" in Africa? To many people it is perceived as a foreign import, and its minions are seen as unable or unwilling to become acquainted with cultural values or supportive of local people. To many people, Christian worship is foreign worship – unless reinvented in the thousands of Independent Churches; Christian symbols are foreign symbols; and Christian ways are foreign ways. In a continent of participatory celebration and manifest embodiment, Christian liturgy is often perceived as pale, listless, and uninviting.

These and other concerns should not be minimized. The fact that they do not tell the whole story does not justify anyone's overlooking their importance: people's hopes and dreams – and people's lives – are involved here. And where lives are at stake, a church that claims to be the vehicle of salvation cannot rest.

A number of hard ethical questions urgently arise for anyone in Christian ministry in today's Africa, for anyone preparing for such ministry, and for anyone responsible for the training of such ministers. As we gathered for the Consultation in Tamale we were conscious, not only of our commitment to inculturation, but of the danger of inaction or inappropriate action and of our responsibilities to other ministers, whether in action or in training. We asked: how can we teach tomorrow's missionaries and ministers, knowing what we do about the current atmosphere of distrust and confrontation between some members of the church? How can we naïvely discuss and write about inculturation as if there were widespread understanding, encouragement, and support of the project? How can we respond most effectively – as Christians – to those who oppose inculturation? How do we ourselves direct our own loyalties: to God, to the church, to pastors, to local communities, and to individuals? It is no easy task.

In Ghana, one of our number referred to all the current talk of inculturation as "a strategy for postponement." There are times when it feels exactly like that. Another was concerned that even the language of inculturation is often interpreted as exploitation, imposition or dictation by local communities, rather than a commitment to walk together to discover how to be better Christians. A third reminded us that inculturation requires *living* together and not simply travelling together: if we do not live with people then we don't understand them, or how they are human, or how they are religious. One of the women at the Consultation put it simply and well when she said: "At the heart of it all is relationship." That indeed expresses both the strength and the weakness of the theory of inculturation, both the potential and the disappointment.

So, there are legitimate concerns to be addressed; yet if it is unhelpful simply to remember the Ghana Consultation nostalgically, it is no less unrealistic to look forward with naïve optimism. What we need is hope. Hope is the Christian virtue of steadfast faith in things unseen but promised. It is, in the words of Cameroonian theologian Eboussi Boulaga, "the dream of the waker." We are called to stay awake; but we are also inspired to dream.

Inculturation, as the process whereby the faith takes flesh in specific times and places, is a matter of urgency. Yet it cannot be rushed, or enforced, or controlled by committees, any more than can any process of organic growth. It has been compared to giving birth: messy, painful, and somewhat undignified – but life-bearing.

Anthony J. Gittins, C.S.Sp.
A Caussé, France
September 9, 1999

INTRODUCTION

LIFE AND DEATH MATTERS

Anthony J. Gittins, C.S.Sp.

In a powerful and challenging essay entitled "The Gospel as Prisoner and Liberator of Culture,"[1] Andrew Walls reminds us that theology at all creative times is "about *doing* things, about things that deeply affect the lives of numbers of people. We see something of this already in South African Black Theology, which is literally about life and death matters."

Matters of life and death are the topic of this book. But we are also reminded that life *matters*, and death *matters*; indeed it is because life and death matter, that inculturation is such an important concern. We are human beings, incarnate, and our existence is a celebration – or a denial, avoidance, tolerance or fear – of life and death. Whatever our attitude may be, it is always the case that life and death matter, in their ordinariness and predictability, just as much – so our faith reminds us – as the more dramatic and unpredictable "matters of life and death."

This book is intended primarily for ministers and pastoral agents actually involved in inculturation, actually working at the interface of faith and culture. It is written and presented in such a way as to be used as a text for graduate students of theology and ministry. Each chapter is rounded off with five questions for reflection and discussion; they may help in the context of an academic seminar. But there is also a real hope that serious non-specialists will use this book: after all, inculturation is something that challenges everyone, and everyone has a contribution to make. Perhaps reading this book will provide some clarity about the practical implications of inculturation, and some sense of the urgency of the agenda.

Thanks are certainly due to the Society of the Divine Word, to the *Tamale Institute of Cross-Cultural Studies (TICCS)*, and to Jon Kirby, S.V.D.: the first of these underwrote the costs of the Consultation; the second provided us with an excellent venue; and the third was our tireless organizer. Further thanks are due to all who participated, both by sharing written submissions and by their creative insights. But thanks for the following pages are particularly due

---

[1] *The Missionary Movement in Christian History* (Maryknoll, NY: Orbis Books, 1996), Chapter One. This has been revised and reprinted on several occasions, most recently in James A. Scherer and Stephen B. Bevans (eds), *New Directions in Mission & Evangelization, 3* (Maryknoll, NY: Orbis Books, 1999), 17-28. This reference is to p. 24.

to the individual writers. Not only did they offer papers initially at the Consultation, not only did they rewrite them after the Consultation, with a view to publication, but they graciously acceded to my request for editorial privileges. In order to bring this book to completion it was necessary to standardize the format of chapters so that the finished product would, as much as possible, cohere. To this end, headings and discussion questions have been added, and style and content have been edited – sometimes slightly and at other times substantially.

One temptation has been resisted: the temptation to cover the theoretical aspects of inculturation in a comprehensive way. Other books and articles are devoted to that, and many are identified in the pages that follow. But insofar as this book is used as a textbook, it will obviously be necessary to supplement it with other works, both theological and anthropological.

It may be helpful to provide something of an overview and a rationale for what follows. **Chapter One** (Anthony J. Gittins), *"Inculturation, the meaning and the challenge,"* lays the terrain on which the other contributions will build. It identifies the theological and anthropological meaning of terminology that is central to this book, and tries to sketch in a preliminary way the pastoral challenge involved in inculturation. It characterizes several approaches to inculturation, so that readers may better understand the intentions and outcomes of its agents; and it acknowledges and emphasizes that the scope of inculturation is nothing less than the whole of life and existence.

We then move into the case-studies: nine attempts to identify and respond to issues in contemporary African life. In **Chapter Two**, *"An unacceptable agape among the Tiv of Nigeria,"* Adrian Edwards immediately confronts us with the problem of a traditional religion in "advancing decay": how should we proceed? In one of his fine essays, Robert Schreiter[2] offered us a very clear statement about the need for the church to affirm cultures in situations which call for *cultural reconstruction, cultural resistance* or *cultural solidarity;* and equally to stand up courageously to situations in which injustice is part of a culture's identity. Here Edwards is pointing out that not every culture is a strongly-blooming flower, and that inculturation is no simple matter: using the horticultural metaphor of a graft, he points out that not every graft is successful.

In **Chapter Three**, *"The family model in ecclesiology: a model from Ghana,"* Edward Tengan illustrates one of the challenges of translation: how

---

[2] Robert J. Schreiter, "Inculturation of Faith or Identification with Culture?," in Scherer and Bevans, *op. cit.,* 1999, 68-75.

to balance gains and losses when we give and take across cultures. The connotations and denotations of the English word *family* are not precisely the same as its nearest equivalent in the *Dagara* language of Ghana. Yet in the latter case, understandings of kinship and affinity, consanguinity and adoption, commensality and community, can be extremely helpful in constructing a local theology of church. Tengan's chapter repays a careful reading and has implications for much further afield than Ghana.

Chapter Four is entitled *"Tswana religion and Christian inculturation."* Ireneo Barreto introduces key terms and players in the traditional religious culture of Botswana, presenting a "worldview and philosophy of life [that are] coherent, perduring, and worthy of attention." In 1975 Pope Paul VI stated memorably in *Evangelii Nuntiandi:*

> Evangelization loses much of its force and effectiveness if it does not take into consideration the actual people to whom it is addressed, if it does not use their language, their signs and symbols, if it does not answer the questions they ask, and if it does not have an impact on their concrete life (n. 63).

Well said, simply true, and often forgotten. Another statement by Paul VI that bears remembering is found in the Encyclical *Octogesima Adveniens.* Referring to the legitimate autonomy of local churches, he acknowledged:

> In the face of such widely varying situations it is difficult for us to put forward a solution which has universal validity. Such is not our intention, nor is it our mission. It is up to the Christian communities to analyze with objectivity the situation which is proper to their own country, to shed on it the light of the Gospel's unalterable words (n. 4).

Barreto tries to keep thoughts like these alive as he considers the importance of the Supreme Being, the family, ancestors and healing, among the *Tswana* people he serves.

The next contribution, from a Tanzanian pastor and theologian, is **Chapter Five,** *"Inculturation as living faith: Bukama, Tanzania."* The imposition of any force or coercion is inconsistent with Christian principles, so the actual experience of his *Luo* parishioners is the starting point for Laurenti Magesa. He concentrates on funeral customs and their implications. The ecclesial model of Small Christian Communities (SCC), adopted as a policy in the 1970s, is judged inadequate: these failed to produce dynamism and social action because they were insufficiently rooted in and responsive to the lives and needs of the people. The author is discouraged to see that "the spontaneous localization of the Christian faith in popular religiosity" is viewed as a distortion by some in authority. Asking not "who holds ecclesial authority?", but "how are the Gospel demands for freeing people being fulfilled in our communities?", he reminds us that the community is theologian, and he recalls the place of the *sensus fidelium* in the life of the church.

In **Chapter Six**, *"Popular problem-solving and inculturation in Dagbon, Ghana,"* we again start from the axiom that doing inculturation in Africa begins with African problems. Literally, in this case. Based on extensive and intensive research over many years, this chapter offers some of Jon Kirby's anthropological and theological insights. Local people who become Muslim feel that Islam shows interest in their own traditional problems, but people who become Christian are perceived to be joining a church that knows little and cares less about their traditional problems – though it does offer advantages in addressing "white man's palaver." Noting that "foreign" attitudes are often supremely irrelevant to people's local experience, the author challenges the church to greater responsiveness to people and their needs. He shows what these needs include, and how the local church is trying to address them. How to be both *Dagomba* and Christian is the issue for the local community; how to be both universal and local is the issue for the institutional church. The chapter concludes with an illustration of, and a theological reflection on, three local social realities: divination, bad death, and witchcraft, showing that though inculturation is not without risk, nor is it an option but an imperative.

"Baby rituals, ritual baths, and baptism: a case from Congo" is the title and topic of **Chapter Seven**. In his treatment, Piet Korse harmonizes the *indigenizing principle* and the *pilgrim principle*[3]: the application of the former ensures that Christianity takes seriously – and absorbs – some of the values it encounters in other cultures and peoples; when the latter principle is applied, a local church becomes converted and transformed by the novelty and challenge of the Good News. This chapter is as rich in ethnographic detail as it is in creativity: each needs the other if inculturation is to proceed. Reasons of space have curtailed it here, but we are given a real taste of where the process might lead. This chapter describes a church of the people, a people's church: it is alive with vignettes and bursting with promise.

Kofi Ron Lange is an American who received a Ghanaian name. In **Chapter Eight**, *"Inculturation and proverbs from Dagbani, Ghana,"* he modestly helps us to see why: proverbs may be the subject of his research but people are the subjects of his ministry. And the people accepted and incorporated one of his own aphorisms as a proverb! He observes that people make themselves known through language, and he shows how language-in-use is a special form

---

[3] See Andrew Walls, *loc. cit.,* 21-23.

of language, different from language-in-texts. He explains that "knowledge of the meanings of innumerable proverbs becomes part of a storehouse of wisdom that is passed down from elders to their juniors." With that in mind, and recalling the pedagogy of Jesus, the author urges us to pay much greater attention to the proverbs that already exist, to learning and being taught by the wisdom they contain, and to discovering ways in which new proverbs – Gospel wisdom – can be added to the storehouse and transmitted to the next generation. Proverbs are not handled lightly and not appropriated by everyone. They are used by significant people: the elders. So unless we involve the legitimate proverb-tellers in our catechesis – rather than simply collecting or stealing proverbs ourselves – we will not only fail to show respect for people and their culture but will miss a great pastoral opportunity for inculturation.

The subject of language and its employment is at the heart of **Chapter Nine**, *"Tears a-plenty: songs of suffering in Central Africa."* The author is Xavier Plissart from France, and the chapter is a superb illustration of *organic progression* or incremental, spontaneous inculturation, as well as an eloquent invitation to other ministers and pastoral workers. Stemming from the life and death of Bishop Munzihirwa, a movement among the young people of Bukavu (former Zaïre) helped to sustain and express the Christian faith in a situation of violence and bloodshed, by producing hymns of great power and theological richness. The chapter echoes a cautious note: if spontaneity can produce heroes and great wisdom, what may happen when routine returns? This chapter shows the enormous potential of a courageous leader and the – possibly unexpected – fruits the Holy Spirit can lavish on a trusting and imaginative community. The power of the blood of martyrs is undiminished, and the songs that sprang up as seed are as evocative as Negro Spirituals.

The book concludes, still raising important questions about language, with **Chapter Ten**, *"Religious profession rites as barometers: the Igbo, Nigeria."* Joan Burke reminds us that women are key agents of inculturation, and shows how a study of rites of religious profession not only discloses a developing theology of the vows, but points to a particularly effective way of instructing the broader community. With 50,000 women religious in Africa, profession rites can be a powerful expression of an inculturated faith. Yet these rites are not entertainment: there must always be an element of shock and scandal in lives radically lived in Christian faithfulness. If the Gospel loses its power to shock, it is not being lived but being betrayed. A sign does not have to be accepted by everyone in order to make sense, but it does have to be meaningful and comprehensible. Turning to the use of vernaculars in these rites, the author shows that much work needs to be done to articulate a comprehensible theology of poverty, chastity and obedience in cultural contexts that do not share

Christianity's own understanding of the vows. There is danger here, and opportunity. One of the virtues of this chapter is that the work is replicable: other people can undertake similar research – and perhaps it is time to extend it to communities of male religious – and discover what religious life means to Africa.

The book thus ends. The task remains.

CHAPTER ONE

INCULTURATION – THE MEANING AND THE CHALLENGE

Anthony J. Gittins, C.S.Sp.

Stating the Issue

What is the primary or essential responsibility of the church? There are many possible ways to answer the question: from the theological ("to be the sacrament of salvation") to the descriptive ("to be the community of the faithful, *The People of God*"), to the functional ("to proclaim the Realm of God: to announce and embody the Good News of salvation, to all peoples, in every culture, until the end of time").

And how is the church to undertake and accomplish this responsibility, this mission? There are just as many ways to address this question: they range from the highly formal and deductive to the more informal and inductive, from the "top down" to the "bottom up." According to the first scenario, the (official, hierarchical) church would develop a blueprint for organization, or perhaps a set of rules for membership, and then follow the blueprint or promulgate the rules in any and every particular circumstance. In the second scenario, the church would encourage research and dialogue with different communities, societies or cultures, in order to continue discovering culturally appropriate ways for its members to be authentically Christian.

The more emphasis placed on the former approach, the more the universal church would become standardized and uniform; the more emphasis placed on the latter, the greater the variety and pluriformity would be.

What if a combination of approaches (formal and informal, deductive and inductive, top down and bottom up) were to be attempted? The results might be less than clear or univocal, and tend toward the fluid or even the messy. But since life itself, and human experience, tends to unfold as rather open-ended, fluid, and even messy, such a synthetic approach to the church's mission may not be altogether a bad thing.

There was a time when the church proudly identified itself as always and everywhere (*semper et ubique*) the same. Universality and uniformity went hand in hand, in theory at least.[1] Experiments aimed at local adaptations of

---

[1] There are, of course, noble exceptions, and especially throughout the first millennium. Pope Gregory the Great (590-604) wrote to Augustine of Canterbury, apostle of the English: "I approve of thy selecting what thou hast been able to collect from many churches. Choose from each several

the church to the people, or cultural variation in the expressions of Christianity – one thinks of Matteo Ricci (1552-1610) in China,[2] Roberto de Nobili (1577-1656) in India,[3] or the Jesuit *reducciones* in Paraguay[4] – were short-lived and ultimately proscribed. Such forms of *accommodation* were condemned by Clement XI and other popes of the eighteenth century. One result, not incidentally, was that nascent Christianity beyond the confines of "Christendom" decayed.

Yet this is only part of the story: *inculturation*, by whatever name, has always been the missionary task, the missionary imperative. In order to explain and justify this statement we must first clarify our usage of the word *missionary*. Vatican II famously declared: "The pilgrim Church is *missionary* by her nature" (*AG* 2). The text continues: "For it is from the mission of the Son and the mission of the Holy Spirit that she takes her origin, in accordance with the decree of God the Father" (*loc. cit.*). The decree to which the text refers flows necessarily from the Creator who is self-giving. So not only can we say that the church is missionary, but God too is missionary. We might gloss the word missionary in this sense, as both "having a mission" and "being sent (on a mission)" – or, in the case of God, "being centrifugal, dynamic, in motion." It was St. Bonaventure who, more than a thousand times, spoke of God as *bonum diffusivum sui:* personified Goodness, or Goodness itself, diffused, scattered, or spread everywhere. It is a beautiful and almost untranslatable yet very dynamic phrase, bespeaking an Action-God, a God who reaches out, embraces, encounters and includes: in other words a *missionary* God, a God of mission.

We shall look at the definitions and dynamics of inculturation in due course. Here let us suggest simply that it concerns the way in which God's message is communicated with humanity, given the twin facts of God's transcendence and humanity's cultural and linguistic variety. At that point we might ask: how, in real terms, is God's plan for humanity actually implemented? And our answer, reached by a circular route, would be: through inculturation!

church such things as are pious, religious, and right, and collecting them as it were into a bundle, plant them in the minds of the Angli for their use." *Ep. Greg*, Bk XI: Ep. LXIV, ad Q. 3. In *Nicene and Post-Nicene Fathers*, vol 13: 75 (Grand Rapids, MI: Eerdmans, 1956), 11.

[2] J. D. Spence, *The Memory Palace of Matteo Ricci* (New York: Viking Penguin, 1984); Andrew Ross, *A Vision Betrayed* (Maryknoll, NY: Orbis Books, 1994).

[3] S. Arokiasamy, *Dharma, Hindu and Christian, According to Roberto de Nobili* (Rome: Ed. Pont. Univ. Gregoriana, 1986); J. F. Moran, *The Japanese and the Jesuits* (London/New York: Routledge, 1993).

[4] Philip Caraman, *The Lost Paradise: An Account of the Jesuits in Paraguay, 1607-1768* (London: Sidgwick & Jackson, 1975).

It is necessary to explain and standardize our vocabulary, either because some writers (present company excepted!) tend to use language carelessly or inconsistently, or because of the confusion that may exist in the minds of some readers. Gerald Arbuckle and Aylward Shorter[5] have attempted to clarify and standardize the terminology; I will do likewise.

Culture, enculturation, acculturation: three words that find their home within the social sciences; their technical meaning is encountered there. *Inculturation*, though appearing to belong in their company, is actually a neologism that finds its home within a theological setting. If the sociologists and anthropologists share a common search for an understanding of *culture*, theologians who use the word *inculturation* tend to take the meaning of *culture* for granted, adding to it a specifically theological note. If theologians sometimes too quickly assume that the notion of *culture* is relatively unproblematic, anthropologists remain very slow to recognize the authenticity of *inculturation*. So when and if anthropologists and theologians ever gather for conversation, it becomes necessary to clarify terminology.

On the other hand, if – as is true of the contributors to this volume – both theology and anthropology are part of one's stock-in-trade, then non-specialist readers might find it helpful if various words and ideas are explained.

Culture has been defined as "the [hu]man-made part of the environment" – but there are at least two hundred other definitions on offer; social scientists have spent more than a century refining and disagreeing about definitions.[6] Two points must suffice at this stage. First, human culture tends to be seen as a *work in progress* rather than a clearly-defined, much less a fixed and objectifiable reality: it exists in people and in processes. Second, culture should not be seen simply as the summit of human achievement: sociologically it comprises the heroic and the horrific, the mundane and the munificent; and theologically, it must include both sin and grace.

In the following pages we will frequently encounter the word *culture*. It might be used to address or include aesthetics, values, relationships, rituals

---

[5] Gerald Arbuckle, *Earthing the Gospel* (Maryknoll, NY: Orbis Books, 1990), 17ff. Aylward Shorter, *Toward a Theology of Inculturation* (London: Geoffrey Chapman, 1988), 4ff.

[6] For example, Tim Ingold (ed.), *Companion Encyclopedia of Anthropology* (London: Routledge, 1994), 151, 368, 474-5. Definitions include: "A body of premises carried by a system of symbols" (D. Schneider); "A web of man-made significance" (C. Geertz); and "A set of adaptive strategies for survival" (A. Rapoport).

and systems of meaning.[7] It might be understood as identifiable in performance: whether in the form of music, dance or story. It might be thought to be experienced as the *ethos* (the near-tangible actuality of everyday life: the stuff of life: reality) or the *worldview* (the way people sense the world should be: the intangibles towards which they strive: the ideal). Culture may range from poetry to pollution, from mysticism to missiles, from dance to deforestation, and it can include art and religion, meanings and memories, signs and symbols. But however we define or encounter it, culture presupposes some kind of community and continuity: it is not simply the experience or expertise of isolated individuals, and not purely transitory. Culture has been handed on by others from the past, is shared with others in the present, and will be transmitted to others for the future. Which brings us to enculturation, and, in due course, to acculturation.

Enculturation, otherwise referred to as *socialization*, concerns the process whereby people assimilate culture. A newborn child is neither self-sufficient nor yet culturally defined. Gradually, by formal and informal training, by rewards and punishments – but above all by being offered a consistent understanding and picture of the way the world and people should be (a *worldview*) – the child is enculturated to become both a bearer and a transmitter of a culture.

But many things can go wrong: not every culture nor every individual is without flaws, and since human social organization is not the same as the social organization of an ant-hill, there does tend to be rather a lot of variation, whether based upon individual choice, peer-pressure, or the strength or weakness of prevailing norms and sanctions.

Yet many things can go right: creativity is another distinguishing feature of the human community, and societies can *develop* intentionally, rather than simply evolve like the Galapagos finches. It is important for us to understand the component of enculturation that we can label *creativity* or even *conversion*: we are not utterly determined by our culture, our environment, or our history.

When two people, enculturated in different ways – or two different cultural groups – encounter each other, the contact or clash is called *acculturation*.

An individual life can be seen as a progressive acculturation, because people are constantly encountering others, gaining new experiences, adapting and growing. From the cradle to the grave, acculturation is a natural component of social existence. However, it is more noticeable or dramatic when two

---

[7] For a fine discussion, in an excellent book, see Robert J. Schreiter, C.Pp.S., *The New Catholicity* (Maryknoll, NY: Orbis Books, 1997), 29.

very different people or two very different cultures come into contact. Such is the human propensity for domination or self-righteousness, that acculturation is rarely completely painless: either one party tries to gain control, or the other party fears that possibility – and takes counter-measures. If the element of trust can be introduced and built upon, then mutuality rather than hierarchy may prevail, at least for a while. But if trust is broken, or if force or fear should begin to dominate, acculturation is capable of producing horrors like the New World exterminations of the sixteenth century, or their Old World counterparts in the twentieth: from the Americas to the Balkans, acculturation has produced rotten fruit; the deaths of Amerindians and Albanians have been the bitter harvest of distrust and aggression.

Yet that is not the whole story: if the lion cannot readily lie down with the lamb, human beings can nevertheless *learn* to care for each other. They can learn that compromise and exchange can be mutually enriching. They can learn that there may be several ways to accomplish the same goal. Acculturation bespeaks a world of opportunity as much as a world of danger; it is the topic of all the contributions to this book.

Culture, enculturation, acculturation: these are part of the *Ur*-language of sociology and anthropology. There is much more to them than we can address here. But already enough hints have been given to indicate why theology might be interested in the topic – particularly theology as it has developed in recent decades. One of the most exciting issues in theology is the so-called *faith and culture* debate.

Faith and Culture[8]

The faith of Christians, and indeed the faith of Israel from which it springs, can be traced back to God's revelation in history. Because history is related to context – it is *somebody's* history, or the history of some place, or time, or species – we can identify the *context of revelation* as the circumstances or particularities associated with God's self-disclosure whenever and wherever it occurs.

For example, Moses received God's revelation – and as we ponder this astounding reality we can attempt to identify and understand Moses' own social location, which includes his age, status, ethnicity, language and religious experience. In order for God to make sense to Moses, and for Moses to grasp

---

[8] A most helpful recent book, edited by James A. Scherer and Stephen B. Bevans, is *New Directions in Mission & Evangelization, 3* (Maryknoll, NY: Orbis Books, 1999). The title of this volume is indeed *Faith and Culture*, and it is a compendium of some of the best recent writing on the subject.

the revelation he would later transmit, God had to speak Moses' language (literally or figuratively), and Moses had to absorb the message in his own cultural categories.

Or consider the encounter between Jesus and the woman at the well, recounted in John's Gospel (Jn 4). It is clear that the circumstances of both their lives were a critical part of the conversation and its outcome. The interlocutors were certainly not stock characters and the conversation was never platitudinous; on the contrary, the particularities of both are intrinsic to their encounter.

Or again, think of how Matthew and Luke report the Beatitudes of Jesus. Matthew's Jesus says "Blessed are the poor *in spirit*, for *theirs* is the kingdom of *heaven*"; Luke's Jesus says "Blessed are *you* who are poor; for *yours* is the kingdom of *God*." The words in italics may be attributed to Jesus (who, therefore, was either poorly reported or must have spoken on two different occasions to two different groups), or are due to the evangelists' recontextualization of the material for their own particular communities.

Context and contextualization are intrinsic to communication, and specifically to revelation. *Quidquid recipitur, ad modum recipientis recipitur*: whatever is received (absorbed, understood, assimilated), is received according to the capacity of the recipient. But similarly, whatever is uttered, expressed, articulated – or revealed – requires a particular vehicle or language, with its specific forms, idioms, and emphases. All of this is to reiterate that revelation is *contextualized*. But so are faith and culture.

Our faith is our reception of, and response to God's revelation. And just as the revelation is specific and contextual, so it is with our faith: we respond in terms of our own social location in its broadest sense: in terms of who and where we are. And a consideration of that will bring us full circle back to culture.

In the language of theology, *contextualization* refers and applies to both faith and culture, tending perhaps to focus more tightly on the expression of the *faith* response to revelation. *Inculturation* also refers and applies to both faith and culture, tending perhaps to focus more tightly on the *cultural* response to revelation. In effect, the two terms – *contextualization* and *inculturation* – are synonymous. They both became part of the *Ur*-language of theology in the early 1970s.[9]

---

[9] Apart from Scherer and Bevans, *op. cit.,* and Shorter, *op. cit.,* the following are recommended: Peter Schineller, "Inculturation: a Difficult and Delicate Task," *International Bulletin of Missionary Research* (1996), 109-111; and E. Ikenga-Metuh (ed.), *African Inculturation Theology: Africanizing*

Inculturation refers to the way in which particular communities or cultures receive the revelation of the Gospel of salvation in Jesus Christ, then assimilate it and express it. And since human beings are not generic – linguistically, culturally, epistemologically – the expressions of response to the Good News will be many and varied rather than one and the same. This is problematic and unsettling for some, and exciting and challenging for others: but it is not a dangerous new idea; it is the story of Pentecost writ large on the face of the earth.

The agents of inculturation are the Holy Spirit and the local community; if only the process were as simple as the premise! The difficulties encountered along the road to inculturation (a never-ending road for people "on the way") are almost always due to disagreements precisely about the Holy Spirit and the local community: about how the Holy Spirit works and who discerns the Spirit's workings, and about the local community and its identity and authority. Indeed, questions of authority (ecclesial, episcopal, communal, individual) and of tradition (large T, small t, apostolic, cultural) sometimes slow down, undermine, or threaten to destroy the process. Yet despite problems and abuses, real or imagined, the project of inculturation must proceed because it is a work of the Spirit who is making all things new and renewing the very face of the earth.

Each chapter in this book looks at current developments in local situations in Africa. Some developments are more tentative or less publicized than others, and some local situations are more extended and less limited than others. But each author is passionately committed to the authority of the *magisterium* and the authority of the *sensus fidelium,* to church and to local community, to faith and to culture, to affirmation and critique. Every one brings a professional competence to the process of inculturation, and none is so naïve as to accept cultural conventions uncritically, or so self-important as to dismiss church documents impudently. But loyalty to the church must be loyalty to God; faithfulness to the teaching must be faithfulness to the Teacher; and commitment to the community must be commitment to its Creator.

Transforming Everything

When we speak of inculturation we sometimes expand the reference into the phrase "inculturation of the Gospel." We must be careful here, and for at

Christianity (Onitsha, Nigeria: IMICO, 1996). The former is a short article describing the field and several approaches; the latter is a compilation of essays on the theological foundations for inculturation.

least two reasons. In the first place inculturation is a two-way street: a dialogical process, or an encounter, between Divine revelation and human society or culture. True enough, "the Gospel" – as we somewhat loosely say – must be "absorbed" into people's lives; but it is equally important to acknowledge that the church, as bearer of "the Gospel," will also be changed by every encounter with people-in-culture. Every local church is part of the universal church, and all the local churches in the world are comprised of acculturated people from a myriad of cultures, so it follows that more universality (greater depth or intensity, as well as greater extension) means more diversity. In Nairobi in 1975, the World Council of Churches "maintained that the cultural context can disclose something *new* and *original* about the confession of Jesus Christ in particular confessional contexts."[10] Its declaration stated:

> In our sharing with one another we have discovered that the Christ who meets us in our own cultural contexts is revealed to us in new ways as we confess him. ... We affirm the necessity of confessing Christ as specifically as possible with regard to our own cultural settings. ... We have found this confession of Christ out of our various cultural contexts to be not only a mutually inspiring, but also a mutually corrective change. We need each other to regain the lost dimensions of confessing Christ and even discover dimensions unknown to us before. Sharing in this way we are all changed and our cultures are transformed.[11]

Every line of this is heavy with significance. The verbs – *discover, affirm, need* – and the phrases – *new ways, the necessity, as specifically as possible, mutually inspiring / mutually corrective, lost dimensions, dimensions unknown, all changed, cultures transformed* – are quite deliberate, carefully chosen, and immensely challenging. This book could be read as a response to the challenge of that declaration.

But there is a second reason for being very careful if we speak of the "inculturation of the Gospel." To speak only of the Gospel is to risk being much too narrowly understood: the whole of life, of existence, must be affected by and responsive to the Good News of salvation in Jesus Christ. Both "the Gospel" and "culture" can serve to place limits where limits are inhibiting and liberation is required; inculturation must be nothing less than the transformation of everything: of our understanding of, and our response to Gospel, revelation, theology, catechesis, ministry, liturgy, politics, economics, family, enemies, life. And unless we articulate – and extend – this list, we will simply

---

[10] Scherer and Bevans, *op. cit.,* 8.

[11] David M. Paton (ed.), *Breaking Barriers: Nairobi 1975* (London: SPCK; Grand Rapids, MI: Eerdmans, 1976), 22-23; quoted in Scherer and Bevans, *op. cit.,* 8-9.

fail to understand the immensity of range and the depth of hope contained within the notion of inculturation and offered in the invitation of Jesus Christ.

By its fruit we will recognize authentic inculturation. The abundant, sweet fruit – blooming and waxing not only in our own gardens nor simply in foreign fields but in the lives of each and all, for God is indeed prodigal with gifts – includes the following varieties: the personal experience of being evangelized, being touched by a living and healing word; individual transformation by continuous conversion (*metanoia; shub*); collective responses to social sin; a joyful, servant-like, *kenotic* ministry; the committed, counter-cultural witness of our lives; our loving moral support for others; our abiding dedication to learning about, and from, other people; a setting down of the burden of our own self-righteousness; a true desire not to muzzle God's Holy Spirit; the appearance of new forms of church, attentive to local contexts and needs; the response to new demands made on the selfish or complacent; and the coming of age of local churches, faith-fully dedicated to a wider constituency than their own immediate membership. These are just a selection of the fruits of inculturation awaiting harvest.

When lives are shaped by Gospel truth, and when behavior and goals have been modified by reflection on the Good News, then inculturation has begun to bear fruit. So when will it be harvest time? Somewhere, every day, the fields are white: the harvest of inculturation is ripe when the Gospel has become relevant to, yet not compromised by a culture; when it is mature food and real nourishment, not the pap of babies or the pabulum of the toothless; when it has transfused new life into communities, not become domesticated or diluted for easy living. Such engagement with people's lives can *only* occur in concrete relationships and is not found in theoretical connections or intellectual breakthroughs. And it *must* occur, like a good marriage, not only in good times but in bad, not only in richer but in poorer, not only in health but in sickness; and as with marriage, so with inculturation: it has to be as strong as death.

Historically, all of these things have occurred: but not often enough and not widely enough. In some times and places they have not even been tried, and where they have been tried they have frequently failed to be sustained. The contemporary world is in crying need for an antidote to the erosion of faith and the idolization of culture. The antidote is available. It is to be found in a much deeper integration of faith and culture. Its name is inculturation.

Inculturation is not simply *a* way – and not even a new way – of looking at other people's reality. Nor is it a sign of respect for their cultures, customs or traditions. It is not a policy designed to produce a local church. In fact it is not a means to an end. This would be to reduce inculturation to a rational task. Rather, it is both the process and the medium of evangelization. It characterizes a whole attitudinal approach as well as an actual encounter, and includes the fructification that is the sign of fertility. Inculturation can never become uncritical acceptance of a culture, any more than it can become cosmetic adaptation of the liturgy or literal translation of the Scripture. It becomes visible as *something new*: a vital, incarnated Christian community of faith and works; a hitherto unknown or unimagined part of the body of Christ; the revelation of an astonishing new facet of God's infinitely multi-faceted splendor; a gift to the whole church and the whole world; a work of the Spirit in our time.

A Variety of Approaches

It is true that people must be approached and encountered as and where they are: in their own local circumstances and experiences. It is also true that the local community, under the Holy Spirit, is the primary agent of inculturation. But neither point detracts from the further fact that a message is involved, and messages have to be communicated. As to the message: it is not simply some philosophy of our own, but the inspired message of God's revelation. And as to the communication:

> Everyone who calls on the Lord will be saved. [But] how can they call on the one they have not believed in? And how can they believe in the one of whom they have not heard? And how can they hear without someone preaching to them? And how can they preach unless they are sent? (Rm 10:13-15).

St. Paul's questions are our own. So those who set out to encounter others and to respond in a kindly, well-intentioned way, have no authority simply to "live and let live," as it were. And local communities, though primarily responsible for inculturation, have no authority to "make it up as they go along," as it were. The Holy Spirit is in charge, and God's revelation is at stake. Inculturation needs some careful approaches and skilled agents.

There appears to be no dearth of material on the nature of inculturation – the issue of *what* it is about. But the record is more patchy on the actual implementation – the issue of *how* to accomplish inculturation. This book is an attempt to address the *how* question; but we can also identify some current approaches, which people may find helpful for their own ministry. They can be discerned in the following chapters but are not necessarily named as such. Those discussed here are: prescriptive inculturation, dynamic equivalence, creative assimilation and organic progression. A fifth, synthetic approach may also be suggested. The approaches could be presented differently, such as *prescriptive* (magisterial), *incremental* (spontaneous), and *intentional* (Spirit-led), or perhaps *ecclesial* (the whole community, indigenous and expatriate), *indigenous* (exclusive of expatriates), and *experimental* (artificially limited to small groups), and others. My presentation here attempts to reflect the most common approaches with a legitimate pedigree.

Prescriptive inculturation is explicitly identified by Laurenti Magesa in the context of his discussion of parish life in Tanzania. It means just what it sounds like: inculturation that is prescribed, legislated for, enjoined, decreed, imposed or controlled. These words are not synonyms, and each shows a slightly different nuance. But they share a common element: they refer to something from outside or above, rather than from inside or below. It would be quite unhelpful to caricature church leaders or ecclesiastical authority, and that is not intended here. And it is most important to acknowledge that inculturation concerns the deposit of faith, the church, the pursuit of truth, and the exercise of Apostolicity. The church does have authority, and appropriate inculturation will require constant loyalty to it. But by the same token, authority must be exercised in appropriate ways. Authoritarianism is not a legitimate style.

What are the strengths and weaknesses of prescriptive inculturation? Its greatest potential lies in its capacity to maintain unity: if the central teaching-office or *magisterium* is responsible for mandating and approving all initiatives, then heterodoxy and fragmentation should be minimized; prescriptive inculturation *may* be an effective means of standardizing or universalizing changes in the church. Unfortunately, such unity tends to manifest itself as lock-step conformity or bland uniformity, which rather undermines any putative commitment of the church to diversity or respect for cultural forms. Because prescriptive inculturation does not proceed authentically from the local church (bishop and faithful), it proves not to be of deep or lasting value. The concern to avoid heresy or the dilution of doctrine, and the fear of making mistakes tend to show through attempts at prescriptive inculturation, thus producing gloom or apprehension where clarity and trust are required.

A sad casualty of prescriptive inculturation is popular religion or religiosity. This is people's very self-expression: the religion of the people. But "official religion" comes to be in tension with "popular religion" (one thinks of the iconoclasm that followed Vatican II, the trivialization of "devotions" both personal and liturgical, and the confusion in the lives of so many who felt bereft of their favorite saints and scorned for their "simple piety"). Where prescriptive inculturation is the order of the day, popular religious forms are either belittled or driven underground. In both cases, people suffer; the church suffers. Inculturation must affect practice and produce living faith: these cannot be made to order or produced by decree.

Dynamic equivalence[12] is the second clearly marked path leading to inculturation. Its starting point is Christian teaching, practice, or liturgy – as found, for example, in the lives of those who first bring the Gospel to a new place, the Decrees of Councils, Canon Law or the Roman Ritual. Dynamic equivalence – like creative assimilation – has been explicitly focused on the liturgy. But inculturation is not so limited.

Starting with the Roman liturgy then, in its *editio typica* or canonical Latin form, a form of translation – though not a literal translation – is made so as to express in other vernaculars, *and in other cultural forms,* the essential message to be conveyed. Since no two languages name and conceptualize the world in identical ways, dynamic equivalence implies a careful search which in fact presupposes knowledge of *both* the Roman Liturgy (and its "culture") *and* the target community and culture; otherwise the translation will be incomplete or even meaningless.

In order to test the success of dynamic equivalence, one could compare it to formal equivalence: the word by word or piecemeal translation. Those who cling to every single Latin word (or even to the words of the English text) and insist on finding an equivalent in other languages, practice such formalism. That approach incorporated words like *Eukaristi, Bredi, Waini, Priesti, Sacramenti* and so on, into an *approved* translation of the Eucharistic Liturgy in a West African country. It is *not* an example of dynamic equivalence.

What are the relative merits? At its best, dynamic equivalence makes sense to the recipients in a way that is also faithful to the meaning of the original message. It is in fact the very heart of appropriate translation: anything less than a *dynamic* equivalence is not a genuine equivalence. And yet if something is gained in translation, something is also lost. Not every word, every precise nuance, every context-bound shade of meaning can be transposed; that is the price of dynamic equivalence. But if the guardians of orthodoxy jealously guard every jot and tittle, their satisfaction will be at the cost of other people's understanding and assimilation. Dynamic equivalence is tested particularly in the matter of figures of speech, metaphors, idioms, and so on: the richness of a language is stored in these vaults. If a local community

---

[12] For this, and the next two approaches, Anscar Chupungco is the best guide. See his *Cultural Adaptation of the Liturgy* (Ramsey, NJ: Paulist, 1982); *Liturgies of the Future: the Process and Methods of Inculturation* (Ramsey, NJ: Paulist, 1989); *Liturgical Inculturation: Sacramentals, Religiosity, and Catechesis* (Collegeville, MN: Liturgical Press, 1992), and many other articles and chapters.

is encouraged to discuss, experiment and modify, and if it is trusted to collaborate internally and with the Holy Spirit, wonderful possibilities await both community and church. But if dynamic equivalence is also *prescriptive*, and if the local community is not involved in its own creation of meaning and significance, the results will be blighted fruit indeed.

Beyond the translation of texts, dynamic equivalence offers great potential and some risk. How do we – indeed, *do* we – "translate" bread and wine, liturgical vestments (or even liturgical ministers), into a thousand different cultures? How do we "translate" gratitude and thanksgiving, sorrow and repentance, joy and excitement, in places where people kill a cow, cover themselves with ashes, or ululate? Here again are issues addressed in these pages.

Creative assimilation is almost the mirror image of dynamic equivalence: it starts with cultural practices that are not already part of the church's tradition, and attempts to endorse them and to gather them into the barns of the People of God. It is based on the assumption that the spark of divine creativity animates every culture, and that God can be worshipped and encountered in myriad ways, many of which have not yet been stumbled upon by those raised in a Western tradition. The *Maasai* of Tanzania anoint people, not with water or oil but with cow fat; the *Shona* of Zimbabwe bury their deceased twice, the second burial being more significant than the first; and in Central Africa a fly-whisk often accompanies a chief.[13] Creative assimilation would start with such behaviors as these, and find a way of including them in Christian practice. This has indeed happened in these three particular cases; but the same is not quite true of many other African rituals. Neither the Cameroon Mass nor the Zaïre Mass really begin with local cultural realities but with at least one eye on the Roman Rite. True creative assimilation would produce *something new,* not something that looks a little like a Roman ritual in fancy dress. An acute problem in Africa, and illustrated in almost every chapter of this book, is encountered by anyone who actually tries to implement creative assimilation in a prevailingly unsympathetic official context.

But those who persevere will be rewarded: commitment to creative assimilation will reveal to them many Biblical texts to support their work and to be appropriately recontextualized for their own situations; study of creative assimilation historically will likewise provide enlightenment on ways of taking

---

[13] I observed the *Maasai* case in 1989; the *Shona* case is reported in Aylward Shorter, "Inculturation: Win or Lose the Future?," in Bevans and Scherer, *op. cit.,* 63-4, citing the Zimbabwe Catholic Bishops' Conference, *"Liturgy for the Second Burial,"* 1982; and use of the fly-whisk is incorporated into the Zaïre Mass.

elements from local cultures and reinterpreting them in the context of the Biblical story of salvation. Only gradually, by experimentation, and with lively trust in the Holy Spirit, will local communities succeed here.

The landmark Roman document of 1994, widely referred to as the *Fourth Instruction*,[14] says some encouraging things, but qualifies them almost to the point of negating them. It gives guarded approval but then adds "as long as," "provided," "on condition that" (n. 40-42), before unequivocally reiterating a statement from *Sacrosanctum Concilium* (*SC* 23), the Vatican II Constitution on the Liturgy, that "innovations should only be made when the good of the church *genuinely and certainly requires them*" (n. 46; italics added). It can hardly be said by anyone who has read it, that the document conveys trust and confidence in local bishops and communities, or that it encourages their joyful and creative response.

The document appears to confine inculturation to formal liturgy. In warning against liturgical abuses it is implicity warning against any attempts at inculturation beyond the liturgy. It states: "the process of inculturation should maintain the substantial unity of the Roman Rite" (n. 36), and that such adaptations as are made "do not envisage a transformation of the Roman Rite" (n. 63). And yet, as we will see, Africa is producing native – if hybrid – fruit, which in the opinion of some theologians deserves to be called inculturation.[15]

Organic progression is the fourth method of inculturation. It represents an endeavor to allow for some novelty, either by *supplementation* or by *continuance*: the former adding to, and the latter extending or elaborating on previous liturgical forms. *Sacrosanctum Concilium* provides the *locus classicus* for organic progression: "Care must be taken that any new forms adopted should in some way grow organically from forms already existing" (*SC* 23). Local churches may find that this offers both opportunity and justification for further promoting inculturation. Prudence is of course called for, but there does appear to be room for interpretation, in respect of how communities grow "organically" as church. Again, throughout the pages that follow can be found encouraging signs of what might be done: some of our authors carefully assess the needs of their local church and attempt to discern how organic progress can be made, using the *editio typica* as the starting point; others appear to start with the criterion for innovations ("[only] when the good of the church genuinely and certainly requires them") and creatively apply it to local churches and particular needs.

[14] Congregation for Worship and Sacraments, *Instruction: Inculturation and the Roman Liturgy.* (*Origins,* April 14, 1994, 746-56).

[15] Aylward Shorter, in Scherer and Bevans, *op. cit.,* 54-67. This reference, p. 63.

And finally, a *synthetic approach* to inculturation would deliberately re-frain from privileging any single method, and would also seek to apply any and every method to as wide an area of Christian life as possible.

The Richness of Human Culture

We looked at a handful of definitions of culture, but otherwise we have taken culture more or less for granted as a crucial component in inculturation. But definitions sometimes state *what*, without explaining *how,* or indeed *where.* In this section, rather than itemize the components of culture[16] and try to give them a theological twist, I will try to indicate how inculturation will employ the forms, the idioms, and the creative diversity of culture.

The Gospel: Today's Not Yesterday's News

If the Word is to become flesh and dwell among people; if the Good News is to be articulated in such a way that people can truly understand; if Jesus the Christ is to become a brother and a Savior to a family that has not yet met him or is not quite sure who he is; if the Gospel faith is to be inculturated – then the old story, and sometimes the old familiar story, must come alive within communities, giving them a better reason to live, urging them to greater things, encouraging them to increased responsiveness to local and global needs, and helping them to deeper reflection on the Living Word and the Living Christ. The Gospel, in other words, must engage with people's actual daily lives.

Proverbs, poetry, songs – and even gossip – can generate local wisdom that may be compared to and challenged by the words of Jesus. And if some of those words have been edited or forgotten, softened or rejected, there can be rediscovery and revitalization as they are juxtaposed with traditional wisdom.

In a globalized world, cable television and the Internet, videos and DVDs provide access to major cultural themes or tropes. The Good News can and should be brought into communication with the daily news, and the promise of revelation compared with the promise of globalization, so that Gospel and Revelation may find a resonance in people's lives, and that people may know an alternative to the dreams of secularization and commodity capitalism.

---

[16] An attempt at a systematic, practical approach to inculturation, applied to Kiribati (an island state in the Pacific), is Anthony J. Gittins, "Kiribatizing Christianity: A Local Church Rediscovers Itself," *Mission Studies* XVI-2, 32 (1999), 71-99.

People speak in vernaculars and think in familiar terms. But they are aware of the existence of foreign languages and perhaps different modes of thought, which can feel unfamiliar and alien. If the church speaks a foreign language – verbally or symbolically – it will reinforce people's unfamiliarity and alienation. Good news has to be told in an intelligible way – otherwise it is, at best, *someone else's* good news. Inculturation *demands* that the church speak with the world – and with people of every culture – in a *mutually* intelligible way.

The Liturgy: The Work of the People

Liturgy is neither arcane ritual nor stylized performance: it is the work of people bent upon worship of God and the creation of community. As we have emphasized, people are specific and embodied, not generic and disembodied. Liturgy is not just *for* people but *by* people. It must resonate with the people: their lives, their experience, their aspirations. None of this is to suggest that liturgical celebration must pander to people or become fashionable or whimsical: but it must communicate with people, and inspire them too.

Vatican II called famously for the "full and active participation" of the community in the liturgy. The liturgy is not a performance staged by some for the benefit of the many, nor is the community cast in the role of passive observer. Christians generally, and perhaps Catholics in particular, need continuous training and encouragement in order to live the liturgy. But people of many cultures have never lost the spirit of community, and a thousand television and videotape documentaries remind us of how people across the world sing and dance, weep and wail, in orchestrated spontaneity and creative chorus. Dance and song, participation and celebration are the stage on which their life's drama unfolds.

Since people vary so much culturally, so also "full and active participation" inevitably varies. On one occasion it might involve total silence and stillness; on another, apparently unrestrained emotion; on yet another, murmured approval of a leader's action. If this is so for daily life, can it not also be the case for the liturgy, the work of the people?

Inculturation presents itself as a challenge to people of every culture to fine-tune their lives and bring them into greater conformity with the Gospel and the Savior; but people of every culture must find the voice to give praise, the style to worship, and the way to celebrate the liturgy.

The Sacraments: Signposts to Help People Home

A church that reduced the sacraments to seven and standardized their canonical form was a church in control of the world and of people. But ocean voyages led to the discovery of a New World, and of people the church did not control. The distinction between sacraments and sacramentals may have served to remind people of the ubiquity of the sacred, but they were perhaps less ready to acknowledge the sacred as much in the new world as in the old.

Sacraments mark and ritualize some of life's major transitions: some, but not all – and some of *some* people's, but not of all people's. In order for sacraments to be more than marginal or magical, they must *encounter* people, yet they are often celebrated at times or in places that are quite out of harmony with the rhythms of people's lives. One thinks of Baptisms that claim to be about the community welcoming a new member with great joy – but take place after the community has gone home, before it arrives, or with a baptismal party that has no relationship whatever with the local worshipping community. Or Confirmations that are embarrassing and incomprehensible to the participants. The litany could continue.

Inculturation offers breathtaking opportunities for sacramentalizing life itself. Cross-culturally there is a huge range of ritual celebrations for marking life's passages, transitions and memorable moments. In another context, Peter was surprised when Jesus turned his suggestion of seven into seventy-seven: we could surprise ourselves at the number of opportunities, not just for forgiveness but for celebration. Birthing, naming, teething, walking, initiation: these mark the first steps of life. Inculturation offers an invitation for church and people to con-celebrate life. There are chapters in this book which take up the offer. But one thing is certain: unless the ecclesial community and the rural or urban community draw closer, they will fall apart. Moreover, if the life of faith – enacted and performed through the sacraments – is not integrated with the culture in which it must exist, then it will surely die.

The Witness: A Godly Enterprise (Acts 5:19-21, 34-9)

Life is strewn with contradiction: it was so for Jesus and it is so for us. Sometimes the Christian community is divided by the very things that should unite it: faith, worship, community, custom and the rest. Somehow one must be simultaneously realistic and idealistic, conventional and creative, risk-taking and prudent. It is not easy.

"Inculturation" has been in the air for thirty years and more; the trickle of books, articles and statements explaining its rationale and dynamics is becoming a flood. From Conferences and Councils – Ecumenical, Pontifical, and World Council of Churches – and from Exhortations and Encyclicals, we have official proclamations and urgent calls for action. We also have warnings, prescriptions, and proscriptions. Move from text to context or from word to action and the record is less clear. Some pastoral ministers have been committed to inculturation as unself-consciously as Molière's *Bourgeois Gentilhomme* (surprised to find he had been speaking *prose* for forty years). Some have written of their experiences and experiments. But others have either failed to understand or to undertake inculturation, or have not written about their adventures. And there are those who have attempted to do one or both of these but have been confused, confronted or condemned – perhaps by their local communities, perhaps by official spokespersons of the church. The situation is delicate, even grave.

Attempts to control vernacular translations by limiting them to formal equivalence – virtually a slavish and literal rendering – have broken the spirit of some loyal servants of the church. Such an approach is a travesty of the authentic science of translation, and repudiates or disregards the metaphor or simile, poetry or imagination that is the genius of the target language. A formal translation of "the spirit is willing, but the flesh is weak" (Mt 26:40-1), translated back into English, yielded "The liquor is agreeable but the meat stinks." Perhaps an apocryphal tale, but a warning to the literal-minded.

Change is normally and routinely resisted, of course, even though revolutions ultimately happen,[17] (most) "flat-earthers" die, and Galileo is belatedly absolved for his impertinence! As for ourselves, maybe we can draw again on the powerful words of Gamaliel, and make bold to say that if inculturation is indeed of God, it will endure, proving resistant and even indestructible (see Ac 5:38-9). Our responsibility, meanwhile, is to witness to God's wonderful works, in every time, and among every tribe and people and nation.

It is impossible to do inculturation without paying careful attention to the mind of the church and its current prescriptions; yet is is no less impossible without serious ethnographic research. At the last meeting of the millennium, the editor of *Missiology*, Darrell Whiteman,[18] made a plea for "clear case-studies" which would be the basis for pastoral initiatives. This book contains a handful. Perhaps, in the next decade, pastoral ministers will encourage more people from local churches to take up this challenge as an urgent priority. Without it, any creative theological breakthroughs – particulary liturgical –

---

[17] Thomas Kuhn, *The Structure of Scientific Revolutions* (Chicago: Chicago University Press, 1969).

[18] Catholic Theological Union, Chicago, Meeting of Mid-West Fellowship of Professors of Mission, November 6, 1999.

will build on shifting sands rather than the bedrock of social and cultural human existence.

The Whole of Life: A Transformation into Christ

No part of life is exempt from grace. No part of life is outside the embrace of inculturation. Faith and culture, culture and faith must be engaged with each other, giving life to and receiving life from each other. Culture must never be allowed to compromise or domesticate faith, but faith must never overlook or trivialize culture. The responsibility falls on all the People of God, but in a special way on ministers and leaders. As for the grace: that will be forthcoming and it will be sufficient; we have God's Word for it. But though we must be committed to bringing people's faith and people's experience into a life-giving engagement, we must not forget that the *terminus ad quem* – the end-point of it all – is something unknown to us and unknowable by us. We cannot therefore control the process: it is in God's hands. But we *could* – and it has been done – muzzle the Holy Spirit, at least for a time. There is sometimes a fine line between irresponsibility and paralysis, or arrogance and timidity, and we must tread it carefully lest we slip and fall from the Way.

Everyone is invited – in fact required – to participate in the process of inculturation, because it is the process whereby the faith grows within us as we ourselves grow, and is expressed by us in our own expressions. It is an on-going, never-completed process of conversion: conversion *from,* conversion *to,* and conversion *for;* from sin and from self, to grace and to God, for everyone everywhere. Inculturation is the process by which lives are transformed – whether personal, private and local, or social, public and global. It requires programs to train people, contexts to facilitate dialogue, challenges to stimulate experimentation, opportunities to form new attitudes, and commitment to undertake personal and communal conversion. That is why inculturation is so demanding, so difficult, and so delayed.

QUESTIONS

1. "Inculturation, by whatever name, has always been the missionary task, the missionary imperative" (p. 20). Discuss what this means, who is included, and the implications of this statement for development and change in the church.

2. If culture must include "aesthetics, values, relationships and systems of meaning" (pp. 21-22), can you suggest topics and areas that might need further attention in the future – both in general and with reference to particular cultures?

3. Examine the Declaration of the World Council of Churches (p. 26) and discuss its significance for expatriate missionaries and local pastoral agents.

4. Several approaches to inculturation are addressed in this chapter. Examine each of them carefully, discuss possible examples, and identify strengths and weaknesses.

5. The actual implementation of the task of inculturation is not without its problems, both intrinsically and in relation to ecclesiastical authority and local circumstances. What is missing from this chapter? (We have not addressed modernity.) From your own current perspective, what other considerations need to be attended to? How will you proceed?

CHAPTER TWO

AN UNACCEPTABLE AGAPE AMONG THE TIV OF NIGERIA

Adrian C. Edwards, C.S.Sp.

This short chapter contains some significant insights about what may or may not constitute inculturation, and about the appropriate conditions for its success. Inculturation, the author argues, depends on a relatively vibrant culture, as well as on the presence of Christian ministers with deep respect for and real knowledge of a local culture. Trendy adaptations are a travesty of inculturation, and good intentions are inadequate qualifications for the immense undertaking we call inculturation.

The Context

Let me indicate the setting of my attempts at inculturation. I was an anthropologist before I was a missionary, and my first fieldwork – among the *Ovimbundu* of Angola in 1955[1] – was done when I was a layman. More than a decade later I was among the *Tiv* of Nigeria as a missionary, and was asked by Bishop Murray of Makurdi (like myself, a Spiritan), to make an anthropological study. I also found myself engaged in making translations into *Tiv*.

The bishop felt that the Catholic missionary efforts among both the *Igbo* and the *Tiv* had failed to produce "adaptations" ("contextual theology" and "inculturation" were children of the seventies). He wanted me to produce "adaptations" which would have a catechetical value, in presenting Christianity to the *Tiv* through their own culture. In my own opinion, what this would seem to require was a relatively stable culture, with a symbolic language which could, without too great difficulty, carry Christian meanings.

Thus I was not at all keen on the bishop's proposal. The traditional religion seemed to be in a state of advancing decay, but for me the main blockage seemed to lie not so much in *Tiv* culture but in the majority of the Catholic missionaries themselves;[2] their knowledge of the *Tiv* language was

---

[1] The book resulting from this, A. C. Edwards, *The Ovimbundu under Two Sovereignties*, (London: OUP for the International African Institute, 1962), looked at the role of the Catholic Mission among the *Ovimbundu*, from the social rather than from the cultural perspective.

[2] This was reflected in the nature of the first Catholic communities in what became Makurdi diocese. They were largely composed of *Igbo* government servants, traders, and their families, who

quite poor: a point which I did not fail to make to the bishop. However, after some experience of fieldwork, I did draft proposals for a catechumenate, in the air at that time, following the Second Vatican Council. There were to be three steps in this, of which the actual baptism was the final. The first was to be the entry, after which the catechumens – who, it was assumed, would remain distinctive groups in the local worshipping community – would be "learners". On passing into the second stage they would be expected to do a certain amount of witnessing to their faith, taking part in outdoor prayer services for example.

The Agape

The novelty of the scheme was an *agape* or shared meal, using normal *Tiv* foodstuffs: pounded yam and "sauce" – soup with a meat, fish, or vegetable base. Those who could participate were the catechumens, and those of the baptized who from the point of view of church law could receive Communion. Those who had not as yet entered the catechumenate or who, having been baptized had contracted marriages not recognized by church law, were to be excluded from the *agape*.

*Agape*s in the early church[3] were ordinary meals, at first linked to the Eucharist but later held apart from it as an occasion when well-to-do Christians could show hospitality to the poorer ones. My proposed *Tiv agape* was intended to strengthen the bonds of faith and charity in the worshipping community, but it was also intended to prepare the catechumens for Holy Communion, and to deepen the Eucharistic understanding of the baptized.

The *agape* was to have been joined to a prayer which identified those taking part as *Tiv* and expressed their gratitude to God for guiding them as a people (certain Old Testament echoes were intentionally present). The prayer stated that the meal was being taken as a sign of their unity in love, and as a preparation for the Eucharist.

While myths about *Tiv* origins existed, and the *Tiv* themselves were very conscious of being a people different from all their neighbors, there was no all-*Tiv* ritual center, or cycle of rites. The *agape* would not have invented a *Tiv* identity, but it did propose to relate the *Tiv* experience of people-hood to the history of salvation.

---

spoke English. Even the early *Tiv* converts tended to be schoolboys who attended all-English-language Catholic schools.

[3] *Agape*s were an element of early Christian worship and togetherness. See F. L. Cross and E. A. Livingston (eds), *Oxford Dictionary of the Christian Church* (London: Oxford University Press, 1997), 26-27; and A. G. Hamman, *La vie quotidienne des premiers chrétiens* (Paris: Hachette, 1971).

This brings me to another point. The main class of *Tiv* rituals, the *akombo* rites, have sometimes been perceived as "sacrifices" because they involve the killing of animals. In fact these rites contained no idea of gifts made to a higher, non-human power. The *akombo* cult groups were indeed "communities of affliction", to use Victor Turner's phrase,[4] since they were composed of people who had at one time suffered from the illness or misfortune associated with the *akombo;* but by mastering the rites they had shown themselves to be wizards. Thus they had the right to share in meat meals – provided by people who had been "caught" by the *akombo* – in return for which they would abstain from the mystical cannibalism which was held to be the reason for all human deaths. The *akombo* rites then, could be seen as a kind of anti-sacrifice, buying off wizards with animal meat instead of human flesh.[5]

Without engaging in an analysis of traditional *Tiv* thought which would not fit the present context, I suggest that these beliefs have two very important consequences. First, since everybody is believed to be a victim of witchcraft *(tsav)* and is mystically eaten by the wizards,[6] the absence of an ancestor cult is understandable.[7] And second, all powers, being linked to witchcraft, are seen as illegitimate.[8] Frankly, there is not much in *Tiv* religion, as distinct from *Tiv* ethics, or ordinary social life, on which a zealous "inculturator" can build. The traditional religion of the *Tiv* has anti-sacrifices in the space where one might expect sacrifice; and, while the *Tiv* are sensitive to eating and drinking together as a sign of friendship, the idea of covenant meals as a consecration of friendship is not marked. It is true that there is a custom – *ihambe* – in which

---

[4] Victor Turner, *The Drums of Affliction: A Study in Religious Processes among the Ndembu of Zambia* (Oxford: The Clarendon Press, 1968).

[5] The position taken by all my informants was that the *akombo* (a term which applies variously to certain cult objects; to the ceremonies performed to "mend" or "rejoice" the *akombo;* to the physical or social condition ascribed to a particular *akombo;* and to the whole complex of objects, beliefs and ceremonies) were linked to the power of the *mba tsav,* the wizards. The same applies to the *swem*-pot, used for oath-taking, which was not regarded as *akombo.* It should be noted that Paul and Laura Bohannan (*The Tiv of Central Nigeria* [Ethnographic Survey of Africa, London: International African Institute], 1952) deny this. But the S.U.M. missionary Eugene Rubingh (*Sons of Tiv,* Grand Rapids, MI: Eerdmans, 1972) seems to hold the same view as I do.

[6] I say "wizards" and not "witches," even though in everyday life women may be more often suspected of witchcraft than men. In the *Tiv* ideology of power, the practitioners of power-related witchcraft are men, and therefore "wizards." See Adrian C. Edwards, "Seeing, Believing and Doing: The *Tiv* Understanding of Power," *Anthropos* 78 (1983), 459-480.

[7] Adrian C. Edwards, "On the Non-Existence of an Ancestor Cult among the *Tiv*," *Anthropos* 79 (1984), 77-112.

[8] There were magical beliefs about Mt. Swem (apparently Ngol Kedju in Cameroon), where shape-changing elders were thought to travel to bring back good or ill fortune for their communities. But Ngol Kedju is outside the real *Tiv* area.

41

two men drinking together can pledge friendship; but this does not seem very important, and some people regard it as slightly ridiculous. However, the eating of human flesh with a wizard, by which one becomes oneself a wizard, is central to *Tiv* beliefs about witchcraft and could surely be called an anti-covenant meal.

My purpose in proposing the *agape* was to bridge the gap between the significance of eating together as a sign of harmony and the Christian under-standing of the Eucharist.

It did not seem to me that one could draw on *Tiv* tradition for the image of a sacrifice or a covenant meal. What I was doing was perhaps not incultur-ation if this means translating a Christian value into an already existing cultural practice, but rather a graft of a Christian idea onto existing *Tiv* ways of acting and speaking, by the invention of a *Tiv* agape. The clergy of the Makurdi diocese, at that time overwhelmingly expatriate missionaries, did not like the idea, fearing that the *agape* would be confused with the Eucharist itself.

The Conclusion

Was this experiment altogether useless? I think not. I later drew up the broad outlines of a regional catechumenate. As for the *Tiv*, there were three steps, but no *agape*. The proposal was accepted by two southern Nigerian dioceses. Later on, in northern Cameroon, I also established a catechumenate for the new parish of *Hina,* where I was parish priest, with, again, three steps. This was not so much, I hope, a partiality for the number three, as the consequence of the practical problem of conducting a catechumenate in a parish consisting of a number of "chapels," or, in Nigerian missionary jargon, "outstations." In such a parish it was not possible to follow the French cate-chumenate scheme of a large number of rites, for instance, the "transmission" of the Our Father or the book of the Gospels. With three stages it was possible to group particular rites together in what seemed to me a meaningful way, and to offer the possibility of seeing the catechumenate as a journey.

Insofar as my experiment was a failure, I would suggest that it indicates, not simply brashness or rashness on my part (I was acting in obedience to the bishop), or extreme conservatism on the part of my missionary confreres. Rather, it indicated a state of affairs by no means confined to the diocese of Makurdi: that is, a lack of fruitful interaction between the essential elements of liturgical inculturation, which are a sound theology of liturgy, the anthropo-logical approach to questions of cultural identity, and the lived pastoral experi-ence of Christian communities.

But what was I trying to do? I have said that I was trying to graft the idea of covenant meal onto existing *Tiv* understandings of eating and drinking, and perhaps this is what most inculturators are doing, introducing elements rather than really *translating* between two cultures. Is this legitimate? It seems to me that it would only be illegitimate if we took what might be called a *hyper-Herderian*[9] idea of cultures as being *authentic* insofar as they are static over long periods of time. But, in practice, cultures grow and change, and are both givers and takers of elements from other cultures.[10] Is, then, presenting whatever is new, in the least startling form possible, all there is to inculturation? I think not. I recall von Hügel's[11] point that one of the motives of missionary work is to bring all the cultures of the world, with their varied skills and values, to Christ. But this involves the prior evangelization of at least some of the people who have internalized them (culture is a given). Evidently, this is a process for which there is no quick fix.

Let me finish by quoting a remark of my teacher in anthropology, Meyer Fortes. The last time I saw him before his death, I said, as I prepared to leave, "I always come to you hoping for answers, but I always leave with more questions." "Oh," he cried, "but how can we poor anthropologists give any answers at all? We have to leave that to you, the missionaries."

[9] Johann Gottfried Herder (1744-1803) seems to have been the originator of the idea of *cultures* as distinct from *culture*. See Isaiah Berlin, *Vico and Herder* (Oxford: Blackwell's, 1976).

[10] The anthropologist Pierre Bourdieu (b. 1930) has stressed the "production" of culture through the everyday working activities of a community, and its "reproduction" by the passing on of "cultural capital" from generation to generation.

[11] Friedrich von Hügel (1852-1925) was a Catholic layman and religious philosopher. He made this point in his *Letters to a Niece* (London: Dent, 1928).

QUESTIONS

1. This chapter underscores the importance of a thorough knowledge of local cultures for at least two reasons: to build surely upon those cultures, and to avoid at least the most embarrassing mistakes. In view of this, who should make decisions regarding inculturation: "experts," clergy, ordinary believers ... ?

2. From the material presented in this chapter, identify significant cultural issues that missionaries would need to understand. Do you sympathize with the objections to the *agape* as proposed here?

3. The author suggests three prerequisites for successful inculturation: a sound liturgical theology, a serious ethnographic understanding, and a faith-filled community. Discuss.

4. What do you think about actually trying to inculturate Eucharist rather than simply creating an *agape*-type ritual? What about encouraging new forms or elements for Eucharist? Is there a danger of an uncritical imposition of the Western Eucharist on to other cultures?

5. Edwards maintains that the *agape* was conceived of as a stepping-stone to the Eucharist. Can you think of other cases where Christian doctrine has to be approached by "stepping-stones"?

CHAPTER THREE

THE FAMILY MODEL IN ECCLESIOLOGY –
AN EXAMPLE FROM GHANA

Edward Tengan

*The author of this chapter looks at the meaning and the lived-experi-
ence of "family." In a fashion similar to the later chapter of Barreto
on Botswana, Tengan uses the model of family as a way to understand
the ekklesia. In the second part of the chapter he explains how an
inculturated ecclesiology is able to build upon and transform the
Dagara understanding of family, and how Jesus might be understood
as becoming flesh to dwell among this people of Ghana.*

Introduction

Inculturation (the incarnation of the Word in a culture) has as its exem-
plar the person and mission of Jesus Christ. As Jesus in his incarnation-suf-
fering-death-resurrection transformed our humanity, so the Gospel as purifying fire transforms and perfects human cultures in the process of inculturation, thus liberating them of all that is anti-human and divisive. In this regard,
inculturation and the evangelization of culture are synonymous. This chapter
attempts to develop an inculturated ecclesiology.[1] The experience of the *Dagara*
of northwestern Ghana offers both a case-study and some symbols and idioms
around which to craft a theological reflection on church-as-family. The method
is perforce inductive. The starting-point is an anthropological description of the
Dagara notion of family.

Part One:
Defining Family among the Dagara of Ghana

The English word *family* has no equivalent in the *Dagara* language. The
social unit based on parenthood and filiation is *yir*, a term used to designate
both the physical house and the social house at its various levels. Thus the *yir*
must be explored as we search for the *Dagara* family.

One of my informants, asked to define the house/family (*yir*), replied
rather elliptically, "it is its *kyiiru.*" *Kyiiru* has a double meaning. Its primary

---

[1] For a summary, see E. Orobator, "Perspectives and Trends in Contemporary African Ecclesiology,"
Studia Missionalia 45 (1996), 267-281.

denotation or literal meaning is "injunction/prohibition" or "[something] forbidden to eat." But it also connotes the "non-human members of a given social house among the *Dagara* who are normally taken from the physico-religious environment of the people."[2] Another name for these non-human members is *dume*. In most cases the *kyiiru* is believed to have intervened mysteriously to save the life of a noted member of the community [patri-house][3] from mortal danger. In recognition of their indebtedness to the *kyiiru* for their continued existence, the community is enjoined to regard the *kyiiru* and all its species as siblings of the given patri-house.

Kyiiru, seen variously as savior, sibling and injunction/proscription, is constitutive of the patri-House. Not only do the members of the patri-House owe their continued existence to its historic salvific intervention. It is also a source of identity for its members. People who otherwise would have considered each other complete strangers immediately recognize each other as kinsfolk through their shared *kyiiru*. Again, the injunctions that come with the *kyiiru* give a specific spirit to the patri-House, to serve as the bond of unity for its members and the source of its specificity as a house. Through the *kyiiru*, the patri-House transcends the normal horizontal relationships that characterize human beings. The element of transcendence is seen, first of all, in the fact that the *kyiiru* are ascribed suprahuman existence. Besides, the *kyiiru* links the living members of the family and the ancestors.

The ancestors link the social house and the physical house to each other and to the transcendent. The *Dagara* believe that the land of the dead is very similar to the land of the living. Hence, each patrilineage has its main house in the land of its deceased forebears: the terrestrial houses are only "temporary sheds." At death, we go home: those who have lived according to the injunctions of their house and thereby contributed to its up-building here on earth will be recognized by their ancestors. The ancestors will see their own image in their descendants and welcome them home. Though dead, the ancestors still retain their interest in the continuity of their house, to the edification of which they contributed in their life. Living by the injunctions (*kyiiru*) makes one a true relative of the ancestors, which is the prerequisite for entry to the main house.

For the *Dagara,* the primary meaning of house is social. One's house identifies the web of social relationships established by paternity and filiation.

---

[2] Edward Tengan, *The Social Structure of the Dagara: the House and Matriclan as Axes of the Dagara Social Organization* (Tamale, Ghana: The Victor Series, 1994), 23.

[3] I use *patri-House* in reference to the broadest level of inclusion within the *kyiiru*. This distinguishes it from the lower level, which comprises people who actually do things in common [*patri-house*]. The terms *clan* and *patri-clan* I use for social guilds comprised of members of a matrilineage.

This all-encompassing social house is the *yir* or *yiilu*. Only by extension does it refer to the physical house or habitat. Actually, the *Dagara* identify four levels of relationship within the patri-House: the broadest level or patri-House (*yiilu*); the patri-house (*yir*); the segments (*logr*) within patri-houses; and the nuptial room (*die*) of the married people[4] within each section. At the broadest level – which encompasses all who belong to the patrilineage and share the same *kyiiru / dume* – *Dagara* talk of house as *yir* or *yiilu*. The main point of reference here is the *dume / kyiiru,* and a person is recognized as belonging to the *yiilu* by sharing the same *kyiiru.* Next is the level of the *yir* which includes all who "still do things in common" even if they live far from each other: the uniting factor is some common forebear regarded as ritual founder of the house. He is the link to a physical house, which represents the much broader social house of the total patrilineage.

Most extended houses are made up of segments or households, of two to four generations living under the headship of the senior male. Such segments (*logr*) are identified by the name of the family head. The symbolic center of a segment is the main granary. People of the same segment till the same farm (land) and eat together. Finally, each married couple within the segment of a house is entitled to some privacy. A young man intending to marry should put up a room for himself and his prospective wife. This room (*die*) is the smallest unit of the house, but its main purpose is to symbolize the house itself and its future. Though *Dagara* expect a man to be in solidarity with his patriclan, couples deserve some privacy.

In the course of history *Dagara* patri-Houses have also experienced processes of fission and fusion. Fission is often justified by explanations which may be mythical, economic, social or ritual. Sometimes the separated segments treat each other as distinct households, while in other cases they cling to their common ancestry. For example, whilst they may see no problem in inter-marrying, they may continue to have the same *kyiiru* and to participate in each other's rituals. Hence, though each segment claims autonomy in terms of ancestry and the regulation of daily affairs, they never lose sight of the things that unite them; notwithstanding the fission, they share a common ancestry and would readily fuse with segments of remoter patrikin rather than join with households with whom they have no such relationship. Constant fission further confuses the understanding of the term patri-house, for a person could talk of his patrikin as comprised of all who share a common ancestor however remote, but the term might also be used in reference to the members of his segment alone.

---

[4] Though the *die* can refer to the nuptial room, the word can also refer to a composite of several families – much like the *logr*.

In summary, though the notion *yir* is the closest translation of the English word *family*, the term is also polysemic: we have to consider the context to discover its reference and signification. It can refer to the total patri-House (*yiilu*); a patri-house (*yir*); a segment of the house (*logr*); the married couple's bower (*die*); or even their offspring (*die*). For the *Dagara*, all these levels are interconnected and ultimately form one reality. The house is built up by marriage and procreation, and the solidarity of the members of the same house is cherished.

Marriage and the Building-up of the House

The *Dagara* house is not static; as the environment for the generation of life, it is itself living and dynamic. Hence *Dagara* talk of the need to continually build up the house. *Dagara* value marriage as a means of personal and mutual completion, but they also view it in connection to life; marriage is only meaningful when seen in the context of the propagation of human life for the patri-house (*yir*). Thus, a childless couple or a couple which produces only girls who will eventually marry out are regarded as useless, because they do not contribute in any way to the continuance of the patrilineage.

Patrikin Solidarity and Relationships

To the *Dagara*, family solidarity refers principally to the solidarity among the patrikin. This can never be sacrificed for any other relationship, not even conjugal. *Dagara* say "a bad brother is better than a good wife." An important maxim in traditional ethics is "you must always support your brother against a stranger." This solidarity extends to co-responsibility in matters concerning the welfare of the patri-house (*yir*).

Family solidarity is symbolized in the figure of the family head, usually the oldest male, the "first-man-of-the-house" (*yir dang doo*) or "house-tender" (*yir daana*). Not only does his age make him close to the ancestors and best able to commune with them, but wisdom is expected to increase with age. Wisdom is required for tending the house. As leader of the household, the house-tender controls the economic, social and ritual activities, with the sole purpose of building up the house. His is the task of ensuring the peace and harmony the house requires for its perpetuity, and for this he counts on the cooperation of all within the house. His rule is not autocratic; he should consult all adult males in the unit before taking decisions that impinge on community living.

Besides marriage, which creates relationships between families, households within a neighborhood are joined together by a variety of socio-political and religious relationships, including joking relationships, ritual pairings, relations established by common membership of earth cults, and so on. Because of these multiplex relationships established by kinship, marriage and residence, it is difficult for a *Dagara* person to come into a *Dagara* settlement as a complete stranger; there will almost always be a common social field. When *Dagara* prescribe hospitality to the stranger as an important value, it is both a way to honor putative relationships as much as a way to practice openness to the wider human community.

Strictly, the stranger (*saan*) would be someone without a point of entry into *Dagara* society: *saan* comes from *saa,* "to appear." The stranger is someone unexpected whose sudden appearance is fascinating. *Dagara* say it could be the supra-human appearing in human form to test the generosity of human hosts. Hospitality is highly valued. Recognizing the liminal position of the stranger, the community seeks to integrate him or her into the social discourse by the prescription of hospitality. In this way, society respects the human value of the stranger and overcomes the problem of otherness.

Part Two: An Inculturated Ecclesiology

From the *Dagara* worldview sketched above, I shall now identify the terms and idioms we need in order to develop an inculturated ecclesiology. As analogical pointers they cannot fully explain the mystery and significance of the church; but by bringing together *Dagara* experience of house and the transcendent reality of the church, I may discover insights about the latter that will be of significance for *Dagara* Christianity and the wider church.

Christology: Jesus Our Redeemer and Brother (dume)

As the Church draws its life and mission from the life and ministry of Jesus, so ecclesiology must be based on christology. Hence, two related questions need to be tackled as the essential prelude to our discussion of the church as a house of God: first, who is this Jesus of Nazareth; and second, of what significance is his life and ministry for us today? Certain christological themes must be kept in mind as we choose an idiom for our ecclesiology: the divinity and humanity of Jesus Christ; Jesus as redeemer; and Jesus as Word of God. The idiom we choose should enable us to talk meaningfully about these truths relating to the person and ministry of Jesus the Christ and open up possibilities of seeing how the local church can be a sign and witness to the people in their concrete situation.

In *Dagara* experience, the figure of the *dume* of the patri-house[5] is the most appropriate idiom for representing the relation between Jesus Christ and the church as house of God. Not only does this image present us with an analogy for speaking about the person of Jesus Christ who is both human and supra-human (divine); it also enables us to reflect on the salvific significance of Jesus within the house of God. As our brother, he makes us sons and daughters of the same Father through his Spirit. And in the notion of injunctions (*kyiiru*) which is related to the *dume,* we have a way of introducing the Christian belief in Jesus as the Word of life, the wisdom for life, and the source of the Spirit that bonds together the members of the house of God.

Figuratively, like the *dume* of traditional households, Jesus came to the rescue of humans when they were in mortal danger and incapable of redeeming themselves from spiritual death. Jesus did not save humanity merely from physical death; salvation liberated humanity from slavery to the powers of evil. In the world of the *Dagara,* one thinks of the *dume* in the context of the fear of witchcraft (*kontome*) and other spiritual ills that prevent people from experiencing the fullness of life. Then one marvels at the fact that Jesus not only sustained the human family in existence, but by liberating humanity spiritually he became the source of life in its fullness for all members of his house. Thus, associated with the members of the house as the source of their life, he has become one of the household. And he is also the eldest brother (*yeb*) within the house and should be accorded all the respect due to the first-born of our human family.

Dagara believe that the original intervention of the *dume* was not simply fortuitous. Likewise, as *dume* of the house of God Jesus makes a deliberate, calculated, and providential intervention in the world. He is the icon of the Father. He is in the Father (Jn 14:9), and thereby shares the divinity of the Father. When Jesus our *dume,* already divine, humbled himself to enter our history and become one of us, he also vested our human nature with divine dignity. If Jesus in his humanity discloses God, he also elevates humanity and makes it possible for everyone to share his relationship with the Father. Jesus invites all those who would join him in doing the will of the Father, to membership in the new family of the elect: the church. Membership is neither by physical birth nor by legal adoption but by faith and rebirth through water and the spirit (Jn 3:5). The task of the members of this new house within the

---

[5] We saw that *dume* refers to non-human members of the local community, typically the patri-house. *Dume* is a loan-word from the *Sisala*, among whom it means spirit/soul. Spiritual beings and ancestors would seem to be potential *dume*.

larger human family is to bear witness to the kingdom and to strive to bring all creation under the rule of the Father.

Jesus is not only the icon of the Father in his person. In his words of wisdom, Jesus also reveals the will of the Father of the house for all the members. In his teachings and exemplary life, Jesus communicates to the members of the house the injunctions (*kyiiru*) they have to live by[6] in order to have fullness of life and to maintain the house in perpetuity. All who listen to his teachings and emulate his deeds will find their way to their main house with the Father. The divine wisdom, the *kyiiru* of the house of God, is summed up in Jesus' commandment of love: "you shall love the Lord your God with all your heart, and with all your soul, and with all your mind, and with all your strength. [And] you shall love your neighbor as yourself. There is no other commandment greater than this" (Mk 12:29-31; cf Lk 10:27-28).

The practice of this law of love (*kyiiru*) identifies members of the house. In listening to the Word through following the injunction to love, the members of the house become bonded in the same Spirit of love who motivates and propels them to live by the wisdom of their Father. They also participate in the preservation and building-up of the house. In this mission the Spirit is the motive-force, and people respond by helping build up the house as a true community of love modeled on the community of the triune God.

Church Structure as Multi-level Patri-house

This understanding of the patri-House serves very well in the presentation of the church as a community of communities. If the universal church is the house of God (patri-House), then the diocese – the segment of the house that "does things in common" under the authority of the bishop – is the patri-house. Like the patri-house, the diocese is not only defined geographically but by a field of relationships encompassing all those who live in communion with the bishop. Parishes can be seen as sections of the diocese (*logr*) or canonical entities under a parish priest who represents the bishop, but they may also be represented as the various local communities or family units which constitute the subsections of a patri-house. To summarize: the church as community of communities can be seen to comprise five levels or kinds of community. The smallest unit would be the basic residential community, the

---

[6] I use the polysemic *kyiiru* (*dume*/injunctions or guidelines for living) for Jesus as the Word. He is the living Word which is also our guide for living. Insofar as this *kyiiru* is the source of unity for the house, it is also analogically the *ésprit de corps* that creates a "one for all, all for one" attitude. *Kyiiru* thus opens up possibilities for talking of the Spirit we share as believers and members of God's house.

family. The second level is the local community comprised of several families. Then comes the parish community, made up of several local communities. Fourth comes the diocese as a community of parishes. Finally, the universal church is a community of local churches or dioceses.[7] Though the family unit at each of these levels enjoys a certain amount of autonomy, the entire family is bonded by the *dume/kyiiru*, that is, by Jesus Christ and his injunction to love.

Family Celebrations as Sacramental Life

Celebration is a hallmark of African family life. Every socially significant stage of life – pregnancy, birth, naming, adulthood, marriage and death – is marked by rituals and celebrations. These life-experiences combine crisis and grace, and the rites and celebrations that accompany them are means by which a family expresses its solidarity. The festive meal is a very significant element. Conviviality includes food-sharing as a sign of life in common, a sign and a source of unity. Children are taught the value of sharing by being socialized to eat in a community, while the refusal of adults to gather at table indicates a serious breach in their relationships.

The Christian family meal is the Eucharist. Hence, to say that the full participation in the Eucharist is a partaking in the family meal of the house of God is to make a statement with far-reaching consequences for our under-standing of the Church as a house and family. The other sacraments marking the different stages or situations of a Christian life flow from and have their meaning in this family feast, through which the life of the family is constantly engendered. Hence, *Dagara* Christians who take seriously their membership within the house of God cannot see the celebration of the Eucharist simply as an appendix to their private religiosity. A weaving of social rituals with the sacramental life will help people see the unity between daily *Dagara* life and the new life in Christ.

Family Leadership: The Palaver Model

One of the primary tasks of ministry is coordination of effort and purpose. To ensure the smooth coordination of activities and roles within the house, leadership is required. Writing about the authority traditionally attributed to heads of families and the transposition of such authority to Christian leaders,

---

[7] *Dagara* beliefs about the relationship between the community of the living and the dead provide the idioms for elucidating the idea of church. See my book, *House of God: Church-as-Family from an African Perspective* (Leuven: Acco, 1997).

Semporé seems to suggest that the African conception of leadership is an institutionalized domination of the members by the head. It may be conceded that institutionalized authority (responsibility for) can degenerate into power (control over), and that leadership may harden into hierarchy. But Semporé does not explain why there is also abuse of ecclesiastical authority in the West, where equality and individual freedom are very much cherished.

The twin hallmarks of appropriate leadership within the *Dagara* house are wisdom (acquired through experience in life) and communion with the ancestors (seen in the strict adherence to the *kyiiru* of the house). If the leader of the house is called the house-tender and if he wields unchallenged authority, it is because he embodies these moral values and the aspirations of the house. The responsibility of the house-tender is to create a climate in which the unity of the members is preserved through mutual concern for the good of each and all. A bad house-tender would be likened to the servant who thinks his master is delaying in coming and begins to beat up the servants. Such irresponsible behavior risks breaking up the house, and he will be held accountable by his own fathers, the ancestors. A good house-tender is conscious of his limitations and seeks advice through family gatherings. This is what Bujo[8] refers to as the palaver model.

The palaver model would ensure that all adult members of the house of God express their views on issues of common concern. This is vital in order to encourage a sense of belonging and to ensure that decisions are implemented. It is not merely an attempt at democratizing the church as a social organization. Rather, it is the acknowledgment of the presence of the Spirit in the hearts and minds of every baptized person. Through the same Spirit the charisms of each member of the house are tapped and utilized for the building up of the community. Concretely, this means a broad-based consultation of various sectors of the Christian community for major decisions that have to be taken in the church. It also implies a greater involvement of the laity, especially in parish life and administration.

The Church's Evangelizing Mission

The church lives between the historical event of Jesus' inauguration of the kingdom and the eschatological hope of its fulfillment in the *Parousia*. As the new People of God, the church is called to gather all the scattered children of God into the one family of the Father in heaven (*LG* 13). In the interim, when many of God's children do not even acknowledge that they belong to the

---

[8] Bénezet Bujo, *African Theology in Its Social Context* (Nairobi: Paulines, 1992).

People of God, the church is authorized by its Lord and given the power of the Spirit, so that it may grow into the tree on which all the birds of the air can find a place. In and through the church, kingdom values and the unity of all humans should be already operative in human history, even if they are not fully realized until the end of time. One might say that the Church's mission is to gather the scattered children of God into one single house, the house to which they originally belonged. By doing the Father's will, members of the house become one in the Spirit and testify to that unity and intimate union with God which is the source of true fulfillment for all human hearts.

The mission of the church as a house is to be a witness of unity and communion modeled on the Trinitarian communion itself. This communion has to be fostered in two ways: as a bonding of love, of and by the members within the house (*ad intra*); and as a movement of outreach and embrace, which will extend the bonds of love among all the scattered children of God (*ad extra*).

Conclusion

If we are to take seriously the notion that the family is a domestic church, we must discover how to center our Christian life on the family. Traditional societies drove no wedge between the social and moral-religious education of the child. Neither were the celebrations of life divorced from the family context, the very source and end of that life. The present tension between family life and church life is at odds with African life-experience. A lesson can be learnt by those who take the family as the model for church. But this requires that the institutional church acknowledge the critical role of the family in evangelization. *Evangelii Nuntiandi* reminds us of the role played by the family in the apostolate of the laity. The document (*EN* 70) notes that the family has appropriately been called the "domestic church," a title confirmed by the Second Vatican Council. It declares that in every Christian family the various features and characteristics of the universal church should be found. Accordingly, the family, just like the church, must always be regarded as the center to which the gospel must be brought and from which it must be proclaimed. Christian parents who see it as their task to train their children for their roles and responsibilities in society must come to see that this responsibility extends to the religious realm (see *EN* 70-71). Similarly, church leaders ought to see it as their responsibility to help families become believing and celebrating communities, living cells of the local church.

All this may demand a transformation of traditional families, to make them worthy dwelling places for the Spirit of the Lord. The greatest challenge may be to transcend the natural bonds of kinship for the higher bonds of universal love (and for the *fictive kinship* preached and practiced by Jesus, which was to gather everyone into a new family of adopted children of God). The fact that Christians share a Father who is the common source of their lives and the creator of their siblingship within the same house must find expression in their love and concern not only for their Christian brethren but for the entire human race.

QUESTIONS

1. This chapter builds on a rather careful word-study of *Dagara* concepts. How helpful is this approach? What does it suggest about the complexities of the task of inculturation?

2. Are you convinced by the author's attempt to identify Jesus as *dume*? How does it accommodate the humanity of Jesus?

3. Consider the concept of *fictive kinship*. Do you find it useful as a way to evangelize African families and wider communities?

4. In your view, does this chapter succeed in sketching a persuasive ecclesiology? If you were to approach an African community, what insights from this chapter would you find helpful as you attempted to build a local church *and* challenge it to become a missionary church?

CHAPTER FOUR

TSWANA RELIGION AND CHRISTIAN INCULTURATION

Ireneo Barreto, S.V.D.

A young Paraguayan missionary working in Botswana attempts in these pages to combine a scholarly understanding of a changing culture and a responsible approach to the authentic Christian tradition. The first part examines the broad contours of Tswana culture and traditional religion; part two explores the opportunities and challenges facing those who evangelize.

Introduction

The present inhabitants of Botswana form a nation composed of different *Tswana* tribes, and the *Batswana* people have been exposed to Europeans for more than a century. This contact has had a profound impact on traditional life, causing many practices to be modified or even to disappear. Yet despite immense socio-cultural change, some things seem to have survived: traditional belief and thought – or traditional religion – is one survivor.

This chapter will attempt to explain both the survival and the contemporary importance of *Tswana* traditional religious forms, showing how they impact on several other areas of traditional life. Then we might be better able to identify areas of potential dialogue between *Tswana* culture and Christianity, with a view to promoting inculturation. Yet we do not presume to dictate or control the actual process of inculturation, which is ultimately a matter for the local church. The agents of inculturation, as has so often been reiterated, are the Holy Spirit and the local community of faith. *Tswana* Christianity is a relatively new expression of the Christian experience in the life of the universal Church. It is neither fully formed nor a living fossil. There will always be need for reflection, creativity, and loyalty to authentic tradition.

Part One: Christianity and Tswana Culture

A study of the history of Southern Africa reveals the development of Christianity and the institutional church. The missionary movement had noticeable results among the *Tswana*, though evaluations differ depending on whether the starting point is the Christian missionary perspective or that of the local people. By 1870 mission stations had been established among all the larger tribes. The London Missionary Society (LMS) was largely instrumental in establishing Protestant Christianity among the *Tswana*. Most *Tswana* tribes today identify with some form of Christianity.

From a local perspective, judgments on Christianity brought by explorers and missionaries are varied. Some people see it in a very negative light. Others take a more moderate view, recognizing that the lives of pioneer missionaries cannot have been easy, and that the values of literacy, schools, and Christianity itself, are a legacy of generous people who gave their lives for the cause. It is easy, in hindsight, to criticize the mistakes of a previous age, but we should acknowledge the genuine Christian ideals embodied in so many people who lived and died for Africa and Africans.

Tswana literacy is due to missionaries: it brought new possibilities of translating different worlds of meaning. The growth of literacy is tied to the growth of the churches. Still, this boon came at a price: literacy also created divisions between the literate ("people of the book") and the illiterate ("heathen" or "pagan").[1] But an informed understanding of *Tswana* collective representations and of the impact of Christianity demands that we look far beyond the schools and formal education. We must also undertake a systematic study of traditional *Tswana* religion in its context, including its political, economic and social aspects.

Features of Tswana Traditional Religion

The percentage of adherents of traditional religion in Botswana is significant.[2] Given people's formal adherence to Christianity, if this figure is in any way reliable we need to ask how Christianity and traditional *Tswana* belief and thought can engage more appropriately and enrich one another in a process of inculturation.

Tswana traditional religion is not connected to a temple or an organized cult for all. Writing in reference to the nineteenth century, Brown averred that "a religion is there, and it is a strange mixture of the lowest form of animism, with a view of the Most High God that closely approximates to the monotheistic

---

[1] Note how the implications differ sharply, according as one speaks of *illiterate* or *oral*: people without literacy are not necessarily illiterate. Illiteracy is often seen as a lack of something, but "oral" people do not lack literacy: they may simply not need it. More positively we can say that "orality" is a highly developed cultural attribute, which literacy may undermine and cause to atrophy.

[2] David Barrett, *World Christian Encyclopedia: A Comparative Study of Churches and Religions in the Modern World, AD 1900-2000* (Oxford/Nairobi/New York: Oxford University Press, 1982). Barrett claims that 49.2% of a population of 1.5 million people are "tribal religionists," *op. cit.*, 184.

faith of the average Hebrew of early Old Testament days."[3] Currently it can be seen that *Tswana* traditional religion is expressed in a rich set of behaviors, including forms of sacrifice and occasional rites led by specific people. Its most outstanding feature is the centrality of the ancestral spirits (*badimo*): without an appreciation of this essential element we will fail to understand not only the narrowly 'religious' aspects of life but the whole sweep of *Tswana* culture.

Religion is intimately related with the rest of social life and can only be understood in its proper context. By way of illustration: the *Tswana* chief (*kgosi - morena*) is a ruler. During his life he holds social and religious positions of leadership – as shepherd of his people, channel to the ancestral spirits, priest, rainmaker, and judge in matters of sorcery. After his death he becomes an ancestor (*badimo*), and people may pray for his continued guardianship. He also continues to be a central figure in religious and social matters.

Discovering the main features of this traditional religion will demand a consideration of the following: the major functionaries and their particular involvement – starting with the chief (*morena*); the accounts of the origin and destiny of people – including analysis of social structures and socio-religious institutions; the ancestors, their place in the collective representations of the people – and their relationship to the living; and the Supreme Being (*Modimo*) as understood by the *Tswana*. Furthermore, this research will have to be enriched by a demonstration of the relationship of traditional doctors (*dingaka*), traditional healing and medicines, and the nature of sorcery (*boloi*). Though the inquiry might be less than exhaustive, each of these areas or elements deserves serious attention, since a complete picture of *Tswana* traditional religion is impossible to present without them all.

The chief (*morena*)

The chief's recognition as a central figure does not come only from his social or organizational roles but from his embodiment of religious and priestly functions. The people of a chiefdom (*morafe*) are regarded not as belonging to a ruling chief but to his deceased father. The living chief must follow the ways and wisdom of the ancestral spirits (*badimo*). If needed, it will be pointed out to him that his decision is not in line with what his late father would have done. A chief has a constant responsibility to address the needs of the living, and at the same time he has to deal with the spirits (*badimo*); if he were to wrong them, they might withdraw their favors from him and his people.

---

[3] T. J. Brown, *Among the Bantu Nomads: A Record of Forty Years Spent Among the Bechuana, a Numerous & Famous Branch of the Central South African Bantu, with the First Full Description of Their Ancient Customs, Manners, & Beliefs* (London: Seeley, 1926), 91.

Through various ceremonies the chief was recognized as a unique link between the people (*morafe*) and the spirits (*badimo*).

The ancestors of a chief were understood to give supernatural protection to the people for whom they were responsible while they, the ancestors, were alive. The people of the chiefdom (*morafe*) would perform sacrifices and prayers on important occasions to the ancestral spirits (*badimo*) of the chief. The chief was the channel for those sacrifices. His role of tribal priest for all his people is thus easy to understand, as is the reverence that people showed towards him.

Human beings (*motho / batho*)

Tswana tradition includes no formal explanations or accounts of human origins – but there are myths, legends, and stories which concern both the origin and destiny of people. These recount that people originated in the east and will return there after death. *Tswana* peoples also have an elaborate system of chiefly genealogies (which of course need to be understood on their own terms, and not dismissed as spurious historical reconstruction).[4]

People are born into a community where they are enculturated or socialized, gradually learning the implications of belonging to their particular society, being initiated through age-groups (*mophato-mephato*) into adult life, and taking on the responsibilities of *Tswana* living (*mokgwa wa Setswana*). Human death is also explained in mythic terms. Long ago, people were asked what kind of existence they would like. The immediate answer – that the dead should return to earth – was sent to the deity by a chameleon; but the chameleon is notoriously slow-moving, and it spent a long time *en route*. After its departure the people changed their minds and sent a second message by a lizard: the dead should *not* return to earth. The lizard arrived before the chameleon and his request was granted. The chameleon finally arrived with the first message, but too late. So death is now normal and inevitable; people die; and no one returns to earth.

Life among the *Tswana* is seen as requiring social collaboration and cohesion. The ultimate aspiration of traditional *Tswana* adults was to enjoy a long and fruitful life, to die and become a spirit (*badimo*), and to continue their existence as part of the community of the ancestors.

---

[4] The nature and functions of genealogies must be understood by any serious student of culture. For a recent summary treatment, with a solid bibliography, see Alan Barnard, "Rules and Prohibitions: The Form and Content of Human Kinship," in Tim Ingold (ed.), *Companion Encyclopedia of Anthropology* (London: Routledge, 1994), 783-812.

Death (*loso*)

A chief was usually given for his resting-place a site adjoining a traditional courtyard (*kgotla*). Ordinary people were buried in the cattle-kraal of their family-group or ward. Women were buried in the backyard of their compounds, and older people were in charge of interring the corpse. The maternal uncle (*malome*) had responsibility for orchestrating the burial. The body was placed in a crouching position in the grave, with the head facing west.

Many meanings are attributed to these actions. Some people think that the *Tswana* believed in a continuation of life after death. Others think that they performed those practices to equip the deceased for a journey to the world of the dead. There are linguistic indications that life does not end with death: the dead person has only "left," has "passed away," has "gone home," or "is absent." This kind of language draws attention to the centrality of death in traditional *Tswana* culture. But there are still other practices that attest to traditional belief in the communication between the dead and the living.

Ancestors (*badimo*)

The omnipresent action of the ancestors (*badimo*) is a notable feature in *Tswana* traditional thought. The ancestors are points of reference for all living authorities, from the chief (*morena*) to individuals and families. So it is not difficult to understand why people speak of living authorities (*morena*) and dead ones (*badimo*), protectors of the chiefdom (*morafe*) and channels to the Supreme Being (*Modimo*). Ancestors (*badimo*) exercise control over the general behavior of the living, using both positive and negative sanctions. They have power to give good health, prosperity or happiness to those who treat them with respect and obedience. They also have power to punish. The conclusion follows naturally: it is important to have *badimo* on one's side.

What is the significance of honoring the dead today? Some people hold that modern beliefs concerning the fate of the dead were already becoming diversified many years ago, and that today many young people do not even know the meaning of *badimo*. Others claim that Christianity has never really reached the *Tswana* soul. They say *badimo* still exercise significant sway in *Tswana* society, even among professionals or professing Christians.

The Supreme Being (*Modimo*)

Before Christianity, *Tswana* people believed in a High God (*Modimo*), who was to some degree responsive to human conduct. Irregularities among human beings would trigger natural effects such as drought, storms or pestilence.

Modimo would use his power for castigating innovations or departures from established social conventions, by sending wind, cold blasts, or heat, and especially by withholding rain. As for death: where it was not attributable to sorcery, it was taken to be an act of *Modimo*.

The possibility of human access to *Modimo* is a complex issue. On the one hand, *Modimo* is believed to be too remote to be directly approached by humans. On the other, people could approach the ancestors (*badimo*) and, exceptionally, the ancestors might be implored to intercede with *Modimo*. Thus the proper channel to *Modimo* is through the mediation of the ancestors.

In comparing the Supreme Being (*Modimo*) and the ancestors (*badimo*), one can say that the ancestral spirits essentially remain human and retain some of their human characteristics. The Supreme Being (*Modimo*), however, is intangible, elusive, mysterious. There is no plural form of *Modimo*, and all human understanding is analogical and anagogical.

Tswana personal names may refer to *Modimo* in various ways: *Kagiso ya Modimo* (Peace of God); *Tumisang Modimo* (Praise God); *Go rata ga Modimo* (The will of God); *Obusiste* (He has returned [prefix *O = Modimo*]); *Odireleng* (Serve God); *Goitse One* (It is God who knows). One of the most interesting aspects of *Modimo* is the attribution of source or origin (*motlhodi*): this indicates that *Modimo* is not remote from people, for as source or origin (*motlhodi*) he is everywhere, involved in everything, and accessible to the truly needy.

Traditional doctors (*ngaka / dingaka*)

In *Setswana* the verb meaning "to treat" is *go alafa,* and the word for treatment is *kalafi.* Diseases can be treated by a wide variety of medicines or treatments; but what is translated "medicines" in English has a far richer denotation and a much broader range of application among the *Tswana* – from "medicines" for protecting people or their belongings to those which help a woman become pregnant. Knowledge of medicines and their application belongs to specialists who make a living by offering their services. They are called *dingaka* (sing. *ngaka*). *Dingaka* are socially approved purveyors of medicines; but there are also socially disapproved "medicine-men" or sorcerers, called *boloi* (sing. *moloi*). A self-respecting *ngaka* would be insulted to be called *moloi*.

One may ask about the religious status and power of a traditional doctor (*ngaka*), and how he receives recognition in traditional *Tswana* society. The answer seems to be found in the belief that the very first such doctors were taught by the Supreme Being (*Modimo*), and the knowledge thus imparted has been passed on from generation to generation.

Sorcerers and sorcery (*boloi* / *baloi*)

The secret, anti-social, and morally reprehensible use of medicines, especially for causing harm to people, is called sorcery, *baloi*. Those who use them, or who are accused of using them, are deemed evil-doers and agents of sorcery (*boloi*). Sorcery[5] is a malicious use of "bad medicine" against a person whom one hates. Sorcery was also invoked to explain unexpected death or grave problems. If a sorcerer was apprehended he could be driven from his home or village, and even put to death. The best way to deal with a sorcerer was to send him into exile, where he could do no more harm. But those believed to be sorcerers were powerful people, and they might lead long and active lives. Catching and punishing them was a huge problem, and a discussion of that would take us too far afield.

Conclusion

Recently there has been a gradual discovery of African traditional religious themes and values, including prayer, sacrifice, traditional healing and medicine, and traditional authorities like the chief (*morena*). All these have a legitimate place in the religious systems of Africa. The centrality of the ancestral spirits (*badimo*) in *Tswana* traditional religion provides the link between two parts of a religious world, where the living and the dead, the visible and the invisible meet.

In *Tswana* traditional religion one sees a unified conception of life, a unity which embraces the nuclear family, the extended family, the lineage, and the ancestors – and reaches back, ultimately, to the Source of Life (*Modimo*). The *Tswana* worldview and philosophy of life are integrated, holistic, and worthy of our attention. After more than a century of contact with Christianity, *Tswana* traditional religion has survived in many respects, though it has also undoubtedly changed.

---

[5] The French word we translate in English as sorcery (*la sorcellerie*) is sometimes the same as what English refers to as sorcery, but sometimes closer to the English word witchcraft. In a technical, anthropological sense, though the language is notoriously unstable, a working distinction is sometimes made between *witchcraft* as the direct, invisible power exercised (sometimes unconsciously) by the *night witch*, while *sorcery* refers to the instrumental use of artifacts, for evil or anti-social purposes. Confusingly, while English has two words, French has to make do with one: *la sorcellerie*!

Part Two: Challenges of Christian Inculturation

The church claims to be both universal and local. *Tswana* culture – including *Tswana* traditional religion – constitutes the primary context in which the people of Botswana live. With this in mind, this section is an attempt to engage the two dialogue-partners in conversation, and to suggest ways in which the processes of inculturation may most appropriately engage with the life of actual and potential Christians.

Christianity is, *par excellence*, the religion of incarnation. Jesus was a male human being, a Jew, living in a particular society at a specific time; in other words he was *enculturated* or socialized within the context of first century Palestine. Unless we appreciate the fact and process of his *enculturation* we will never fully understand the rationale behind *inculturation*. There are no generic human beings. Everyone is particular, specific. And there is no such thing as culture in the abstract: only specific cultures. Just as Jesus operated within (and sometimes against) the constraints of his particular time and place, so people today and everywhere are called to do the same. Inculturation is the process – complex and multiplex – whereby a particular culture is called and converted to the Gospel, and reciprocally, the process whereby Christianity itself becomes ever more specific by virtue of being born again or incarnated in a particular culture. Inculturation includes not only the proclamation of the Christian message but the construction of local theologies, the renewal of the liturgy, and the transformation of every aspect of life as it is touched by and responds to the Word of Life.

According to Vatican II, culture has a legitimate autonomy and freedom (*Gaudium et Spes* [GS] 59); there is a plurality of cultures; and each person has the right to develop within a particular culture (*GS* 53, 59, 60). People, as social groups, create the culture of their community (*GS* 53, 55).

The third chapter of the Post-Synodal Apostolic Exhortation, *Ecclesia in Africa* (*EA*), addresses "Evangelization and Inculturation." Inculturation is seen as a condition for evangelization. As far as African Traditional Religions are concerned, "a serene and prudent dialogue will be able [...] to protect Catholics from negative influences which condition the way of life of many of them and [...] to foster the assimilation of positive values such as belief in a Supreme Being who is Eternal, Creator, Provident and Just Judge, values which are readily harmonized with the content of the faith" [*EA* 67]. As for the adherents of traditional religions, they "should be treated with great respect and esteem, and inaccurate and disrespectful language should be avoided" [*ibid.*].

The section "Inculturating the Faith," in chapter 4 of *Ecclesia in Africa*, presents the necessity of a "synthesis between culture and faith," because "a faith that does not become culture is not fully accepted, not entirely thought out, not faithfully lived." Inculturation then, is "a priority and an urgent task in the life of Africa's particular Churches." For the Synod "the challenge of inculturation in Africa consists in ensuring that the followers of Christ will ever more fully assimilate the Gospel message, while remaining faithful to all authentic African values" (*EA* 78).

The theme of community illuminates all aspects of the *Pastoral Plan* (*PP*) for Southern Africa. The church is spoken of as "God's community," which indicates the kind of image it "should assume in this part of the world." The *Pastoral Plan* is in fact the result of serious reflection on these matters, and the title – *Community Serving Humanity* – "sums up the many steps [...] to take during the coming years in order to improve [the] way of being Church."[6] The broad task of evangelization covers many areas such as inculturation of liturgy, building lay communities, fostering small Christian communities, and searching continuously for appropriate ways for spreading the Gospel (*PP* 5). The responsibility of evangelization falls on every member of the church, and the invitation of Jesus is offered to every person on earth. The church lives and grows by participation in local communities, and the most intensive form of community building in any region takes place in and through the establishment of small Christian communities. The bishops remark in their "Introductory Letter" that Catholics in South Africa will easily recognize their own life-situation while those from other countries – Botswana, Namibia, and Swaziland – will feel the need to adapt the plan to make it relevant in their own dioceses.

At this point we should identify significant cultural and religious elements where the process of inculturation will be most experienced. The areas I have chosen to examine can be taken as the good soil (see Mt 13:1-9; 24-30; 36-38) of *Tswana* traditional religion and culture, where the Gospel can take root and Christianity can become relevant to people's lives and their deepest aspirations.

The Living and the Dead

Traditional expressions of respect for the ancestral spirits (*badimo*) provide a point of departure for the process of inculturation of the Christian faith. To begin with the social institution of ancestors would be to approach incul-

---

[6] South Africa Catholic Bishops' Conference, "Community Serving Humanity" (Pretoria, 1987), 7.

turation by way of *creative assimilation*: what is wholesome in a local culture is acknowledged by, and organically transplanted into the daily life of a Christian community. Can it be done?

The relationship between the living and the dead forms a *leitmotif* of daily life. The extended family – a basic building-block of *Tswana* social organization – includes the departed in general and the ancestors in particular, as well as the unborn. The ancestors are among the main mediators of life, goodness and wisdom, and constitute examples of responsibility and justice. It was the quality of their lives that made of them *badimo* in the first place. *Badimo* are exemplars of the ethical ideals that permeate society; they form a bridge between the present life and the existence which continues after death. They encourage, inspire, and persuade the living to attend to their responsibilities, and ultimately to confront death with serenity.

Two beliefs or assumptions undergird respectful relations with the dead: the survival of the individual after death, and the reality of communication between the living and the dead. The dead are honored when their names are given to newly-born children, thus assuring the memorialization of the dead and the linking of an as-yet unformed child with an already proven elder. One begins to see already the possible connections between the traditional place of ancestors and the Christian doctrine of the Communion of Saints.[7] Could one not informally call the virtuous dead the "saints of the family," much as one identifies rather more formally the Communion of Saints?[8]

The ancestral rites or service of the ancestors (*tirelo badimo*) were used for establishing relations with the *badimo*. Christianity took the word *tirelo* and used it to translate "liturgy." In *Setswana,* the theological language of Christianity became *tirelo Modimo*, where *Modimo* refers to God. Ironically, "service to God" is an unthinkable notion in traditional *Tswana* religion, because uttering the word *Modimo* is taboo and there is no cult directed to *Modimo*. The phrase *tirelo badimo* needs to be carefully reconsidered therefore, as one continues the process of liturgical inculturation.

---

[7] See Elizabeth Johnston, *Friends of God and Prophets: A Feminist Theological Reading of the Communion of Saints* (Ottawa: Novalis/Continuum, 1998).

[8] Londo Boka di Mpasi, "Antenati, mediatori di vita," *Nigrizia* (Luglio/Agosto 1993), 52-55; also, E. Lapointe, *An Experience of Pastoral Theology in Southern Africa: Inculturated and Committed Christian Communities* (Rome: Pontificia Università Urbaniana, 1986), 51. He proposes widening the circle of family ancestors: "Although we cannot challenge the cult of the ancestors as such – which somewhat resembles our cult of the saints, our fathers and mothers in the faith – we must probably enlarge it, purify it, and give God his place, the first." *Ecclesia in Africa* has recognized in ancestor veneration in African Traditional Religions a preparatory stage for a theological development: "Is this not in some way a preparation for belief in the Communion of Saints?" (43).

It would surely be a gross error to oppose the respectful honoring of the dead, or to encourage its abandonment. That would produce a deep crisis and induce many *Tswana* Christians to lose an integral part of their own identity. The church is challenged to ponder the following question carefully: what would be the best pastoral, psychological and social approach to *Tswana* Christians, in respect of the theme of the living and the dead?

Religious Role of the Chief (morena)

Another interesting arena in which inculturation may be played out concerns the person and role of the *Tswana* chief (*morena*). It is incumbent on those involved in constructing local theologies and promoting the integration of Christian communities to make a serious analysis of the socio-religious role of the chief. One of the reasons for this is simply that the phrase "Lord Jesus Christ" in *Setswana* is *Morena Jesu Creste*. He is "Lord of lords" (*Morena wa barena*), "Chief of chiefs" (*Kgosi ya dikgosi*), "Chief of heaven and earth" (*Kgosi ya legodimo le lefatshe*). In the minds of local people the connotations and denotations must be very strong, and surely a worthy subject for theological reflection.

Tswana Understanding of God

A further arena for inculturation would be the traditional *Tswana* images of the Supreme Being (*Modimo*).[9] *Modimo* is "the only one," "creator," and "source"; his special attributes include mastery and dominion over the cosmos.

The identity of *Modimo* in traditional understanding is quite problematic if one is seeking the *creative assimilation* of this image into an inculturated Christian theology. On the one hand, *Modimo* is the name that was chosen and is currently used for "God" as understood by Christian theology. However, in traditional *Tswana* religion – rather as among the ancient Israelites – this name must not be spoken. *Tswana* Christians today may image God rather differently from the way their ancestors imaged *Modimo*. Nevertheless, given that *Modimo* is employed as the word for God in a Christian context, authentic inculturation demands that careful study be undertaken, in order to ensure that people's understanding of *Modimo*/God is consistent both in terms of Christian theology and of traditional *Tswana* understandings.

Perhaps a basis upon which to build a more explicit theology is this: traditionally, the *Tswana* invariably named their children with an attribute of

[9] Gabriel Setiloane, *The Image of God among the Sotho-Tswana* (Rotterdam: Balkema, 1976), 77-86.

Modimo; every child's name was a reminder of the wonderful deeds of God in the life of individuals and community.

Tswana Human Values

A further focus of inculturation is the human values cherished by traditional *Tswana,* for inculturation is concerned with the evangelization of culture, and culture includes the values characteristically embraced by a particular society.

Traditionally, *Tswana* social institutions were *embedded* rather than *institutionalized.* Institutionalized institutions are those aspects of social structure that tend to be identified as more or less functionally self-contained. Whether any social institution is ever completely free-standing or self-contained is of course highly debatable. However, for analytical purposes we may identify four social institutions: kinship, politics, economics and religion (or belief and thought). Among the *Tswana* these were *embedded* in the social fabric and in each other. In such a world, actual behaviors cannot be analyzed as if they are nested solely within a single, discrete social institution. Marriage for example, though clearly something to do with kinship, is to be understood and explained no less in terms of political, economic and religious themes.

Religion is *embedded* in people's lives, not simply *institutionalized* either in (church) buildings or in (religious) ceremonies. True, religious rites – intuitively or formally defined – mark the most important moments of people's lives. But they are not always religious in the strictest sense, if by that we exclude behaviors more usually identified with other social institutions. Historically, among the *Tswana,* there was no rigid separation of *religious* and *secular* activity, no absolute division between the *sacred* and the *profane.*

Life has a sacred character: it is mystery, awe, created rather than simply crafted. Respect for life is therefore a moral virtue. Giving and sustaining life is appreciated, and that is one of the conditions for becoming an ancestor (*badimo*) after death. Life should be long and honorable. Life does not end with death, and thus the occurrence of death is interpreted in terms of immortality; death becomes a change of state, a journey to a world where the person lives forever.

Individual life finds its meaning in community: "a person is a person with people" (*motho ke motho ka batho*). Participation in community life is also participation in the life of the ancestors; it is not merely secular but also religious. The dead are simply the invisible members of family, ward, nation. Life is intended to be communion: communion with each other in community, and communion with the nation, the ancestors and God. These values embedded in *Tswana* life are entirely compatible with Christianity, and must not be lost when people embrace the faith.

Tswana Traditional Healing

The traditional doctors (*dingaka*) are important ritual figures in *Tswana* society. Some Christians may find it problematic that they act under the direction of the chief (*morena*), but theirs is an essentially ministerial role: they are mediators with the divinity. A traditional healer (*ngaka*) is an institutional channel for receiving the healing that is understood to come from God.

Jesus is referred to as the big – or most important – doctor (*ngaka e kgolo*), the doctor of doctors (*ngaka ya dingaka*), and the doctor of people (*ngaka ya batho*). Jesus is the one who mediates and cures, who has the opportune medicine for every situation, and who in particular has conquered *evil (O kgona mmele le moya*).

In the past, traditional doctors (*dingaka*) were rejected, ostensibly because of abuses and attributions of superstition. Today they are in a phase of rehabilitation. The task now is to find an appropriate integration between traditional doctors and healing, and contemporary (Western) practice. There is something to be learned from both sides.[10] But one thing that must be understood by the proponents of both Western medicine and Christian missions is that in the world of the *Tswana* it will always be as important to discover the social causes of sickness as it is to diagnose and treat the physical. Traditionally, every instance of sickness would be interpreted as connected with the power of the ancestors (*badimo*) or with other supernatural agencies.

The belief that the ancestors taught the first doctors might be the key to understanding that healing can come only from God: God the Creator has the remedy. The idea that death is an act of God underlies the traditional belief that God controls life. In sickness one might initially look for the traditional doctors – and indeed to fail to do so would be regarded as irresponsible. But the last resort – sometimes literally – is God. Prayers will be directed first to the ancestors for enlightenment about the causes of sickness. And the doctor, now enlightened by the ancestors, will also pray before starting the actual diagnosis; he is considered to be an instrument of the divine.

Without negating the values of scientific medicine or the appropriate administration of traditional medicines, inculturation requires a respectful

---

[10] For 30 years the government of Ghana has sustained an exemplary collaboration between traditional healers and Western-trained doctors, nurses and pharmacists.

conversation between Christian theologians and ministers, and *Tswana* healers. It cannot simply be a matter of one system ousting the other; if Christianity purports to address the integrity of persons and society, then it must engage in authentic dialogue about physical, mental, and spiritual life.

The areas addressed here represent some of the main challenges for the church of Botswana. Inculturation is a long and complex process, but it must be undertaken in a holistic or integrated fashion and not simply in an *ad hoc* way; a deep understanding of the worldview of the *Tswana* is required. This is not of course to claim that the *Tswana* worldview is totally integrated and without any elements of pathology; simply that unless one understands inculturation as a kind of transplantation of one living organism into another living organism, one will either harm the recipient or simply botch the operation. At its best, the philosophical and religious wisdom of the *Tswana* is like a web of significations, the various strands of which are interrelated. The task at hand is how to form authentic *Tswana* Christians – people who are truly *Tswana* and truly Christian. When this is accomplished it signals both the conversion of the *Tswana* and the transformation of the church. Like the Kingdom or Realm of God, we could say that this is "already, but not yet." The aim of inculturation is that the Christian faith may become *Tswana*, may become a new creation expressed by *Batswana* in *Setswana*, and that the people themselves become a new embodiment, a new incarnation of the faith.

General Conclusions

In its first contact with the peoples of Southern Africa, Christianity encountered *Tswana* culture through European missionaries. The social location – historical, cultural, theological, denominational – of the missionaries largely determined the patterns of encounter. Though some missionaries were exceptionally sympathetic and scholarly, in general Christianity did not respect and therefore failed to comprehend traditional religion. Recent decades have seen enormous changes in mission theology and in the way Christians approach people of other traditions. Inasmuch as the traditional religions of Africa and elsewhere are currently understood to be the historic vehicles of general revelation (historically therefore, the *normal* means of salvation), the church now needs to promote interreligious dialogue with *Tswana* religion. This might of course be much easier if the latter were codified and formalized, a religion of the book and not (simply) a religion embedded in the fabric of daily life.

What is the future of *Tswana* traditional religion? Is it not destined to disappear? The answer would seem to be no. For the *Tswana*, adhering to Christianity would not necessarily imply a radical break with their traditional understanding. Rather, it could be a new way of seeing the world, a way of encountering persons, places and things that is also part of the genius of *Tswana* life, part of *Tswana*-ness. Commitment to Christianity need neither be a turning to the past nor merely something connected with the dead; it can be relevant for the present and the future and a path to new life.

The British, the French, the Italians and the Germans are allowed to be themselves with their characteristic differences. The world and the church *needs* them to be their authentic selves, for the variety of cultures is of the nature of humanity. We are not generic but specific; and unity does not demand uniformity. And if the people of various nation-states of Europe are not precisely the same as their grandparents, nevertheless they are in some respects closer to the traditions and behaviors of their grandparents than those of their cross-cultural cousins.

So it should be with the *Tswana* people. Traditional belief and thought contributes to psychological and social identity and integration, making it possible for people to understand and value themselves and each other, to accept their condition, and yet to deal appropriately with pain, sickness, and misfortune. Religious traditions and activities may help people to handle the tension between the human person and the invisible world. It is not always possible to separate *Tswana* traditional religion from traditional medicine, for reasons we have seen. More significantly from the point of view of inculturation, it is not always easy to identify or define superstition. This is partly because of the Western propensity to identify it with any mode of action unfamiliar to post-Enlightenment Europeans or with anything not empirically verifiable, and partly because of the theological propensity to invoke Satan or the devil as the likely explanation of otherwise inexplicable outcomes. At least the questions of superstition and of syncretism are in the process of re-evaluation.[11]

If it is difficult to define superstition adequately, so it is a challenge to define *Tswana* religion. We referred to its *embeddedness,* but not only is it embedded in the political and economic or kinship spheres, it is also to be found in many places other than churches and in many behaviors other than those which formally attend to prayer or worship. It may be expressed in conventional behavior, rationalizations inherited from the ancestors, or more generally in immemorial custom: "things believed and done" (*mekgwa ya borraarona*).

---

[11] See P. Schineller, "Inculturation and Syncretism: What Is the Real Issue?", *International Bulletin of Missionary Research* 16 (1992), 50-53; R. Schreiter, "Defining Syncretism: An Interim Report," *International Bulletin of Missionary Research* 17 (1993), 50-53; and C. Stewart and R. Shaw (eds), *Syncretism/Antisyncretism: The Politics of Religious Synthesis* (London: Routledge, 1994).

Of all the characteristics of *Tswana* traditional religion, perhaps the most significant and pervasive is the place of the ancestors (*badimo*): they attest to life after death; they exercise authority and dispense power as agents of the Creator (*Modimo*); they operate as exemplars for the living. As the maintainers of order and the normal controllers of sanctions, the ancestors are the foundation of the *Tswana* worldview, notwithstanding the supreme but somewhat distant significance of *Modimo*. After the recent work undertaken in East Africa generally, Botswana's particular local church must now be taken more seriously. A starting point may well be the place of the ancestors, their significance in contemporary Christian thinking and theology, and their possible location relative to the Christian doctrine of the Communion of Saints.

Life for the *Tswana* is to be lived in community, as a big family – or as we say in English, in "one big happy family." It should be noted that the *Tswana* address as mother and father (*Mme, Rre*) not only biological parents but many of the ascending generation. Does this not provide an interesting point of convergence for those who want to encourage the "big family" of Christians? Would the idea of an extended community not be a helpful analogy when one approaches the sacraments, especially baptism, which are intended to incorporate and sustain people within the great family of Christ, a family that surpasses any actual experience of kinship?

Knowledge of history, ethnography, and traditional religion are all prerequisites of authentic interreligious dialogue. This dialogue must not be delayed any longer. *Tswana* people are known for their capacity for dialogue – familiar in the African *moot,* which is designed not only to bring confrontation to a conclusion but to bring confrontational parties to peaceful and harmonious coexistence. This is actually one of the main functions of the traditional court (*kgotla*). Dialogue therefore, conducted by members of local communities, is what will lead to authentic inculturation. The local church in Botswana is responsible for inculturation of the faith – consistent with the demands of community, in conformity with the Pastoral Plan of the South African Conference of Bishops' Conferences, and according to the Magisterium. 1986 saw the first Diocesan Pastoral Consultation for Botswana. Now this Consultation is carried out progressively. Its declared aim is to provide a vision and to implement a model of church – concretely – in contemporary Botswana. 1993 saw a new Pastoral Consultation Team, mandated to implement the consultation process in the Diocese. In that same year the Diocese of Gaborone produced its own vision of the church: a "participative church." In February 1996, in a pastoral consultation workshop on "A Participative Parish Community in the *Tswana* Cultural Context," the vision was confirmed and further developed, incorporating core *Tswana* values.

The Diocese of Gaborone, in accordance with the *Pastoral Plan* and the later *Special Assembly for Africa*, has adopted as a pastoral priority the initiation and animation of Small Christian Communities (SCC). The priority had actually been adopted in 1984 during the first Pastoral Consultation. But it has received new impulses. One of the basic elements to be taken into consideration in the creation of SCCs is the geographical reality: local cells (*makgotla*) will be organized. This system is in line with traditional *Tswana* social organization, which created small groups or cells around the traditional court (*kgotla*). This new undertaking is a conscious attempt at inculturation by the local church.

Other special *foci* for inculturation include the *Setswana* marriage process and its relation to Christian marriage as well as the rite of marriage, and the inculturation of the liturgy, specifically the Roman Rite of the Mass. But in a country where the majority of clergy and women religious are expatriates, a huge priority – before inculturation can be adequately implemented – is the learning of the language, *Setswana,* and of the culture itself. Cross-cultural formation is an imperative, for unless the ministers of the Christian faith are conversant in "the Setswana way" (*mokgwa wa Setswana*), there will simply be inadequate understanding of, and moral support for the enterprise.

The Catholic church does not stand alone in Botswana's religious field: cooperation among the Christian churches is an important task. A useful moment of encounter for all the churches is at the death of a member who belonged either to a mainline church or to an Independent one (AIC, African Independent Church). But beyond that, church personnel are involved in teams that work in development and charity commissions. It remains a great challenge for the church to address the questions and meet the needs of the people in an African way. Many AICs appear to be doing a better job, and the increase in recruits is a testimony to that. This constitutes yet another area for dialogue and for mutual learning. There is a long way still to travel.

QUESTIONS

1. Discuss the treatment of *Tswana* ancestors as an example of *creative assimilation* (see ch. 1).

2. The author discusses names for God and their appropriation by Christianity. Do you find it adequate? What pastoral and procedural principles would you apply, if you were a pastor?

3. Is it helpful to think in terms of *interreligious dialogue* when Christianity encounters African traditional religions? How would this differ from some conventional encounters?

4. This chapter proposes a model for Small Christian Communities (SCCs). Does this represent an honest encounter between local social forms and the Christian message – or does it seem superficial and cosmetic rather than an authentic basis for an encounter between culture and Gospel?

5. Why is it important for Christian ministers to understand other worldviews? How – specifically – does such understanding contribute to inculturation? What is the implication of the absence of such an understanding?

CHAPTER FIVE

INCULTURATION AS LIVING FAITH –
BUKAMA, TANZANIA

Laurenti Magesa

If the faith is to be truly vibrant, lively, and life-giving, then it must not only challenge but engage with and respond to the daily experience of real people. In this chapter, the pastor of a parish in Tanzania chronicles some of the joys and pains of building up a strong Christian community. An African himself, he has great sensitivity to the needs of African people in a universal church, which is also an African church.

Introduction

Prescriptive inculturation[1] has never been very successful in marrying Christian teaching with African religiosity in the experience of Tanzania. In the 1970s, for example, the bishops of Eastern Africa determined that building Small Christian Communities (SCCs) was to be the pastoral priority of the region: SCCs would be *the way* of being church here. Almost 30 years later some observers note that this aim is far from being realized, not least because of the theological and practical uncertainties of the bishops themselves. But the most basic reason for the failure is that the faithful have not been able to appropriate the notions underlying the policy. They ask: what does it add to our lives of faith? At best, SCCs in Eastern Africa, and specifically in Tanzania, are prayer groups with hardly any element of social action. They are attended not because of the spiritual benefit they engender but primarily because they are a part of the official church's current regulations.

In their study of the problem of inculturation among the *Sukuma* of Tanzania, Ralph Tanner and Frans Wijsen observe:

> The Roman Catholic church in its three dioceses in *Sukuma*land, while [ostensibly] operating under the general policy of inculturation, has failed to do so in any significant way which might have attracted the religious attentions of the *Sukuma*. In fact the church has tended to move towards greater

---

[1] This is exactly what it sounds like: inculturation-by-order or inculturation-by-decree. It describes a top-down approach, or a policy that has been predetermined by people outside a local situation (cf. Ch. One). In common with others, Magesa argues that it does not work.

centralization, enabled to some extent by the easier communication through their wireless network, with a bureaucratic priesthood increasingly detached from its parishioners.[2]

The same authors add:

> If the *Sukuma* are to see the church as providing a place of last resort for them in their difficulties, then it will have to develop a much more personal and outdoor set of liturgical practices. All the *Sukuma* are worried about the fertility of their fields, yet only parish-centered harvest festivals occur. They are worried about the fertility of their wives, so why have such blessings been removed from the liturgy? If they are sick, why is the grace of God not made available to them in their homes as a matter of ordinary liturgical practice? Overall we ask why have so many of these opportunities basic to the culture of the *Sukuma* been surrendered passively to the increasing popularity of their traditional healers?[3]

Similar questions can be asked about the church in Africa in general, and in Tanzania in particular. What is understood as inculturation? What is the dominant approach to the process of inculturation in Tanzania? Does the current approach integrate the various aspects of the religious life-experience of Catholics in the country? If not, which approach does so more effectively and meaningfully?

These are my concerns in the following pages, with reference to a specific context and culture. I live and work among the *Luo* people, north-east of Lake Victoria, and I investigate death, burial, and funerary rites among the people of Bukama parish where I am currently stationed. I address the following question: have these *Luo* Catholics been able to integrate, synthesize, or syncretize Catholic teaching – which has always been hostile to their customs in these areas – with the way they perceive and practice their Catholic faith? After briefly describing traditional burial and mourning practices I shall indicate how Bukama Catholics – and they consider themselves true Catholics – intuitively integrate Catholic teaching with their traditions and practices.

I call this *inculturation as living faith in Bukama,* and relate it here in the hope that one small example of inculturation in a particular place may shed some light on inculturation as a living process elsewhere. But first, some theoretical considerations.

---

[2] Ralph Tanner and Frans Wijsen, *Seeking a Good Life: Religion and Society in Ukusuma, Tanzania* (ms, 1994-1995), 7.

[3] *Op. cit.,* 21.

From Acculturation to Inculturation

As soon as there is contact between people with different ideas, outlooks and lifestyles, a process of acculturation occurs. It is a process of intellectual and social adjustment necessitated by the reality of human intercourse and relationships. Acculturation is a social process that affects whole groups or cultures, rather than simply individuals. Acculturation, or culture-contact, is expressed through linguistic and material symbols and involves the attempt of the parties to enter into each other's world, so to speak – or at least to understand and participate in it to a degree. Since meaning and meaning-making are critical aspects of a group's identity, they are highly significant in the process of acculturation. Each group, while perhaps wishing to understand the other, also needs to retain its identity and integrity.

Acculturation is a sociological term, used in respect of contact between cultures. Inculturation, however, is a specifically theological term.[4] In Bukama, the contact we want to discuss here is between cultural Christianity (Catholicism) and *Luo* culture (and religiosity). This contact has taken place historically in the context of the victimization and alienation of *Luo* religiosity by a form of Catholicism that was Europe-based, and by the process of globalization which has gathered momentum since the beginning of the twentieth century. For Bukama – as for Africa in general – globalization has marked what has been called the black person's "anthropology of misfortune," begun during the slave-trading past and continued by missionary activity. Even though the alienation of African cultures was not always the intended goal of missionary activity (which was to preach the Gospel of Jesus Christ), nevertheless a form of cultural pillage was Africa's actual experience of acculturation, as Christianity encountered African cultures.

Granted that "globalization has created a certain homogenization of the world in its wake," as Schreiter remarks,[5] it has "at the same time unleashed new particularisms, religious protest movements, nativist reassertions of sovereignty, and fundamentalisms of a variety of stripes. These particularisms represent in many instances a new intensification of the local."[6] In Bukama this intensification has been low-key but nevertheless very real in the religious experience of the people. There have been only two major approaches to the inculturation of the faith in Bukama, reflecting the prevailing conditions just

---

[4] This topic is more formally covered in the opening chapter of this volume.

[5] Robert J. Schreiter, C.Pp.S., *The New Catholicity: Theology Between the Global and the Local* (Maryknoll, NY: Orbis Books, 1997), ix.

[6] *Loc. cit.*

described. They manifest themselves in what can be described as *official religion* on the one hand, and *popular religion* on the other. But there are significant differences between these approaches. The former is espoused mainly by religious officials: bishops, priests, religious, and to some extent catechists. It tends to be rather methodical, intellectual and analytic, with emphasis on orthodoxy understood as intellectual assent to defined doctrine. Its approach is hierarchical: "church leadership or its intellectual élite try to move the cultural and religious mixing in a certain direction."[7] Schreiter mentions three strategies that this approach uses to form religious identity. One is "tolerance," or the circumscription of a space in which different possibilities of action exist "as long as they do not produce conflict." Another is "encompassment, whereby church leadership moves to incorporate outside practices and ideas." And the third is "legislation," by which is meant that the Church moves to officially institute certain reforms.[8] The point to note here is that in all of these approaches it is the official Church as described above that maintains initiative, power and control.

At least three strategies may be identified as flowing from the official approach to inculturation. The most extreme of these used to be called the *clean sweep* approach: an attempt to destroy African cultures with their rituals, traditions and customs. Underlying this is a perception of African religion and religiosity in their entirety as pagan and totally incompatible with the Gospel of Jesus Christ.

A second strategy is called *adaptation*. Like the *clean sweep* approach, this is also found in an earlier phase of Western missionary Christianity, especially immediately after Vatican II in the 1960s. Certain carefully selected – and, on the whole, "innocent" – externals of African religion are accepted and modified to fit the official view of church, sacraments and catechesis. *Adaptation* is in effect limited almost exclusively to the use of local languages, local dress, and certain melodies for songs and dances. Elements of much deeper religious significance, such as the existential implications of certain rites and rituals, are simply ignored.

Incarnation constitutes the third strategy: an attempt is made to insert Jesus and the message of the Gospel into African cultures, so that they can be expressed in indigenous idioms and symbols. Far more than the two other strategies, *incarnation* accepts some fundamental aspects of African religiosity as lawful and valid ways for salvation. Nevertheless, the criterion which

---

[7] Schreiter, *op. cit.*, 78.

[8] *Ibid.*, 77-78.

determines these values as lawful remains the interpretation of official theology, in which officially approved Christian intellectuals play a leading role.

Whereas official approaches to inculturation are intellectual and analytic, concerned with correct doctrine (*ortho-doxy*), popular religion is basically intuitive and spontaneous, more concerned with appropriate behavior (*ortho-praxis*). And whereas official attitudes are driven by the need to regulate and even control the life of faith of the people, popular religiosity – which is the actual religious activity of real people – is shaped by the need for balance in life, which is to be achieved by resolving existential tensions or living peacefully with the kinds of inconsistencies, contradictions or even paradoxes which inter-religious and inter-cultural living inevitably produces. This is what the Burkinabe theologian Sidbe Sempore speaks of as

> the very lifeblood of the people, springing from an immemorial source and flowing through the veins of a humanity that is anxious to express its aspirations and to gauge the potentialities and limits of its condition. For a people lost in the immensity of the universe and struggling with all kinds of oppression it is a matter of exorcising fear and anxiety and of reaching a settlement with the powers from above and from below in order to assure a *modus vivendi* based on balances of power and agreements that have constantly to be re-negotiated.[9]

Sempore goes on:

> [T]o speak about popular religiosity and inculturation in Africa today is to touch upon a massive reality, which is present everywhere and in which all sections of African society participate. [...] Notwithstanding the predictions of numerous sociologists, the religious character of the African peoples is far from having evaporated in its contact with technology and modernity. On the contrary, it seems to be regaining its strength and finding a new vitality. Everywhere churches, fraternities and religious movements are flourishing, and the whole of Africa is experiencing a fever of all kinds of religious manifestations, devotions and practices. This phenomenon [...] questions the theological reflection and the pastoral practice of the African churches.[10]

Popular religiosity may manifest itself in a number of ways in its evolution toward authentic inculturation. One of them, described by Schreiter, is resistance: "Because power plays such a strong role in a cultural [-religious] encounter, and because that encounter is often intrusive, unequal and violent,

---

[9] Sidbe Sempore, "Popular Religion in Africa: The Cry of Hope," in J. van Nieuwenhove and Berma Klein Goldewijk (eds), *Popular Religion, Liberation and Contextual Theology* (Nijmegen: J. H. Kok, 1991), 80.

[10] Sempore, *op. cit.,* 73.

the reaction to the encounter is not infrequently resistance. Resistance can take the form of utter refusal to participate, or, if participation is forced, of withdrawal as soon as possible."[11] The numerous African Initiated (or Independent) Churches, which can also be found in Bukama, are examples of popular religious identity formed through resistance to the power and intrusion of the mainline Christian Churches.

The most frequent pattern of what we might call "popular inculturation," however, is the "hybrid" type, which results "from an erasure of a boundary between two (cultural-religious) entities and a redrawing of a new boundary. This has also been called *creolization*."[12] It might also be called syncretism, and is usually regarded with suspicion by the official church because it is seen as a watering down of orthodoxy to fit what are considered to be "pagan" practices and customs.

The problem between official and popular inculturation is mainly that they are exclusive of one another in practice. The issue is one of continuity and discontinuity, convergence or dichotomy between them. Is there or is there not a radical continuity or convergence between the fundamentals of African Religion and Christianity in their perception of God and God's self-revelation? Is there or is there not some common ground between them? Perhaps most crucial of all, as far as practical experience and religious living are concerned: by whom and how can and should this common ground be established?

The official Church – clearly, articulately and loudly – claims the authority to establish such common ground. "Popular inculturation" on the other hand simply assumes it as the people live their lives of faith in the context of their cultural-religious demands. Here the question of who has the power to do what, is not and cannot be very helpful. The question should rather be: what kind of inculturation or "good syncretism" fulfills the Gospel demands of freeing people to be more and more open to the love of God in their own milieu?

Inculturation as Living Faith: The Experience of Bukama

To flesh out the foregoing theoretical considerations, I offer a practical example of popular inculturation as an ongoing expression of the faith of the people, an expression which frees them from the oppressive burden of professing one thing while actively living another. I will relate the experience of Bukama, of which I have firsthand knowledge.

---

[11] Schreiter, *op. cit.*, 73.

[12] Schreiter, *op. cit.*, 74.

Culturally speaking, Bukama is predominantly *Luo*, a Nilotic, non-*Bantu* ethnic group. Religiously, however, it is very diverse, with a significant number of Christian denominations: Catholics, Seventh Day Adventists and Mennonites live together in relative harmony. There are also many African Initiated Churches, the identity and membership of which fluctuates as people move north and south across the Tanzania-Kenya border. But *Luo* traditional religion also attracts the majority of the overall population.

As far as the general faithful is concerned, there is constant contact and mutual influence between all these religious groups. Church hymns are shared across churches, though this is frowned on by officials of the larger denominations such as the Roman Catholics.

In its forms of worship, the African Initiated Church, *Legio Maria*, employs procedures and prayers of pre-Conciliar Catholicism. The *Legio* also treasures Catholic Latin prayer books, rosaries and mass vestments, and takes pride in displaying them. Marriage across the denominations is very common, and does not present itself as a problem for the general population: for some religious groups it is one way of acquiring new members. All of these issues influence Bukama Catholics as they perform funerary ceremonies.

Luo Funerary Customs in Bukama[13]

Wailing constitutes the announcement of death for the *Luo*. There are, however, rules regulating this custom, according to the social status of the deceased, and to the manner and the cause of death. Traditionally, adult men were not allowed to wail for the death of a child below five years of age; if they did so the child's mother would not conceive again promptly. However, all women, including the child's mother, were permitted to wail. But if the child was a twin, no one should wail, and the surviving twin could not approach the corpse – again for fear of infertility.

The ban on wailing also applied in the case of the death of a very wealthy man or a medicine-man (*ja bilo*). The ban remained in effect for one full day after the death. Similarly, it was taboo for anyone to wail when the father of a deceased married man died before that man's widow had been "inherited" according to the rules of the levirate.[14] No convincing explanation is given for

---

[13] The customs referred to here are currently practiced though frowned on by the official church. So some of them are performed clandestinely "when the priest is not looking." (Personal communication, Ed.).

[14] The levirate requires that the widow of a married man without heirs be espoused to a (classificatory or true) brother of the dead man, who makes her pregnant. The child born of this leviratic union – which, in its strict understanding is not a new marriage but a completion of an

this custom, but it was believed that wailing in such instances would somehow interfere with the promotion of life among the living.

A child of less than fifteen years of age was traditionally buried in a shallow grave – dug by a stick carved like a hoe (*mulo*) – close to the parents' dwelling. The type and location of the grave were intended to facilitate the child's "appearance" to the mother in dreams so that she could conceive quickly again. The child's father or paternal uncle buried the male child, while any female close relative took responsibility for the actual burial of a female child. Twins were buried in the same way, except that a female was buried first, on the right side of the parents' bed. This was because she did not belong to the home (*mgogo*), as she would have left it at the time of marriage. A male twin was buried second, and on the left side of the bed.

In the case of the death of only one of the twins, a wooden doll (*orindi*) would be carved for the survivor, for comfort, but probably also to indicate that life goes on. A different location for burial was chosen when a nubile girl died. For fear that she would cause trouble to her family because she had not married in her lifetime, she was buried far away from the houses, outside the hedge enclosing her home. One of two things had to be done in a case like this: if she were to be buried outside the domestic enclosure, the sexual act would be simulated on her, using a stick shaped like a phallus. This was done by an old woman. Alternatively, she could, by consent of a brother-in-law, be buried at his home with the promise that he would be given in marriage to one of her sisters. In this case, the sexual act was not simulated because she was now considered married by proxy.

When a pregnant woman died, the body remained unburied for a full day in the hope that the fetus would deliver on its own. If it did not, the woman's corpse was laid in an open grave which no one – but particularly women of child-bearing age – was allowed to approach until evening. Then, for a promise of a sheep (for a cleansing sacrifice) and a cow (as a gift), an old woman was chosen to enter the grave, open up the womb of the dead woman, extract the fetus, and place it in a smaller grave dug within the mother's grave. Everything else followed in the normal way after this.

On the death of a parent, surviving family members stripped naked to signify that the family was now exposed, bereft, naked. If an unmarried adult died, this custom would not of course be observed.

---

already existing marriage – is the legal offspring of the deceased, who is therefore the *pater*, though obviously not the *genitor*.

On the death of a married man, cattle belonging to his clan members were taken into the bush at the edge of the village and then driven back into the village with much shouting and simulation of war (teng'o). This was to signify the man's bravery. In the distant past, raids were undertaken into the neighboring villages and cattle actually stolen as a sign of bravery. No such performance or war dance was held for women.

Different ritual acts were performed on certain corpses and at certain kinds of death. Thus, mourners would stick thorns into the feet of a deceased barren woman to signify the children she ought to have had. A squawking chicken, signifying a crying child, was held over her grave for a time for the same reason. The back of a deceased hunchback had to be split open with an ax by a marksman in the grave, prior to interment. To fail to do this was to invite bad luck: more hunchbacks would be born into the family and clan. A leper was as a rule not buried, but was placed under a certain type of tree (bondo) which was then felled over the corpse. In the case of a suicide, the Luo uprooted and completely burnt down the tree on which the person had hung himself or herself. If the suicide took place in a house, the house was also burnt down.

Death by drowning was regarded as an evil omen, so the victim was buried at the edge of the water in which the death had happened. A rock was taken from that spot to be buried ceremonially at home in the homestead of the drowned person. Whoever met other kinds of violent death, such as a thief caught in the act or a victim of war, was not buried but was left at the very spot where he had fallen.

The body of a grandfather was made to sit beside the grave and was anointed with oil by the grandsons. It was then wrapped in cow- or goat-skin (sanda) and interred. The senior wife was first to throw soil on the body in the grave with her elbow, to indicate that she had been faithful to her husband. If not, and if she failed to take certain medicines (manyasi) as a precaution, she would collapse and die at the graveside. When a widow died before the levirate rites had been performed for her, someone – we might call them mentally ill – was found to perform the sexual act on her corpse before she could be buried. The same rule applied in the case of the death of a widowed daughter-in-law whose father-in-law died before she had been "inherited."

There were rules governing certain behavior after burial. During the mourning period, which sometimes took a long time, a woman was not supposed to engage in sexual intercourse after the burial of her child and before her next menstruation. A day before the end of her menses, she or her oldest daughter went to her parents' home with some flour. She returned the following day with a chicken, which was promptly slaughtered, roasted and eaten. Then she had intercourse with the husband who could also now resume normal sexual relations with his other wives. Also, after this ritual sexual intercourse, the woman could get rid of the two pieces of wood (*omind diel* or *odier remo*) she had worn since the death of her child. She hid the pieces of wood near the village water hole so that they would deflect the bad luck from her and onto other women who came for water. That is precisely why bereaved women were prevented from visiting the water hole until after the cleansing ceremony (*chola*).

The *chola* ceremony was not required of the mother of a deceased unmarried girl, because the rituals surrounding the burial of the latter (described above) made her a married woman with her own home. In fact, throughout the mourning period her relatives considered themselves visitors and had to be served. On the other hand, a form of the *chola* ceremony was required of a widower whose wife had died during pregnancy. When he dreamt of having sexual intercourse with his dead wife *(oro ne lek)*, he would go to her home and receive a goat or chicken. The next day he would return home, slaughter the goat or chicken, and eat it with his family. He would then resume normal sexual relations.

The senior widow indicated her authority over the family by sitting on her husband's stool shortly after his death. And the oldest son had to be first to have conjugal relations (usually five days after his father's death): that is, before any of his brothers. Sexual activity marked the official end of the mourning period (*ketho liel*) in a variety of circumstances. In the case of widow inheritance, should the new husband fail to complete the sexual act, or if safari ants entered the house during sexual activity, that indicated the dead husband's disapproval of the union. It had to be stopped, and another man would consummate the act. Remarried widows were introduced and accepted in their new homes by the sharing of two meals: the first, of meat, was provided by the new husband at his home; the second, prepared by the woman at her deceased husband's home, was brought by her to the new home to be shared by all present. Otherwise a wasting disease (*chira*) would inflict the families.

The Practices of Bukama Catholics

The foregoing brief but dense description was necessary in order to account for the selective or syncretic processes that have permitted parishioners to remain both Catholic and *Luo*. Due to natural atrophy or social change, some practices have died out or are moribund because they are inconsistent with modern times and new knowledge, but many are still alive and some are quite resilient.

The pastor in a nearby parish outlawed the *teng'o* ceremony[15] as incompatible with Christian faith, threatening to excommunicate anyone who participated in it. A general outcry ensued, for most people failed to see in what way it contradicted Catholic faith. Many simply began to attend services at another parish. As far as I know, the controversy is still not solved, with the priest maintaining his position and a number of parishioners refusing to accept it. Because they see it as an important ritual, they offer stiff resistance to their pastor.

Unless pressed to articulate the reasons for their selective choice of practices to live by, people do not feel the need to spell them out: the selection is more spontaneous than strictly rational. Further, the reasons offered are usually of a practical and not a formally theological nature. Intuitive practice guided by intuitive faith seems primary; logical analysis follows after, but rarely by the majority of the people: that is for academicians.

In practice, apart from the general expectation that Catholics in the vicinity should be present to offer material support and prayers during the funeral, the parents are still accepted as the main actors in the burial of their children: fathers and paternal uncles should take care of the burial of male children and the women of females. Everything happens, in the burial of Christians, in the traditional way we have described above. The activity of the parents and the women relatives is seen as a sign of the strong bond that exists between parent and offspring, a bond that is not expected to end at death. The traditional *Luo* regulations governing wailing are still accepted by Bukama Catholics and are not challenged by them, despite persistent discouragement by some church officials. The assumption that a dead person will appear in dreams and impart a message, is also accepted as normal: no one ever suggested to me the need for a Catholic liturgical service for interpreting the dreams of the faithful in Bukama. Yet my investigation left me in no doubt about the religious importance the people place on these experiences, despite the church authorities' pastoral hesitancy and even resistance.

Most Bukama Catholics accept that a widow should remain sexually inactive until she is joined to one of her late husband's relatives in a leviratic union. This union, they feel, is entirely consistent with Catholic truth. The more knowledgeable people referred to 1 Cor 7:3-5, interpreting it as affirming that prior to the leviratic union the widow still belongs to her deceased husband

---

[15] See above, under *funerary customs.*

and should not give to anyone else what is his right: herself in sexual inter-course.[16] That is why leviratic unions continue among Bukama Catholics despite long-standing and severe censure by the official church. Catholics in leviratic unions are denied the sacraments because they are considered to be living in a state of polygamous marriage.

Many people consider the church's interpretation inaccurate. They asso-ciate leviratic unions[17] with the religious responsibility to care for widows and the poor, and with the importance among the *Luo* of producing offspring to continue the lineage of the deceased. Their argument (or sentiment) is the same as that articulated during a meeting of church leaders at a neighboring parish in 1966, and recorded by Michael Kirwen:

> In the meeting, the African leaders pointed out how the church, in the name of charity, enjoins on all, the support and care of widows and their children, quoting James 1:27. The conflict over this issue, the Africans declared, arises over the question of how one can best help a widow in her needs. The church, they noted, officially encourages the Christian communities to take care of all the widow's needs except that of procreation (*uzazi*). The Africans argued that the widow's procreative needs are as important and as real as her needs for food, clothing, shelter; for it is only through her continuing fertility that she can maintain the integrity and continuity of the family begun with her husband, fulfill her sacred obligation to participate fully in the procreative process, and in addition, look forward to care and support in her old age. The meeting concluded with the statement that the *Luo* leviratic union cannot be construed as either immoral or incompatible with Christian charity, and that the custom should not continue to be proscribed unless it can be clearly demonstrated that Christ himself in the New Testament had forbidden it.[18]

The levirate needs to be public and official; therefore the food exchange and eating together that takes place after the union has been ratified is still valued and practiced. The union is not merely symbolic, and the people see

---

[16] "The husband must give his wife what she has the right to expect, and so too the wife to her husband. The wife has no rights over her own body; it is the husband who has them. In the same way, the husband has no rights over his body; the wife has them. Do not refuse each other except by mutual consent."

[17] The author appears to conflate *levirate* and *widow inheritance*. He writes: "By *levirate* I refer to a widow (with or without children) who is 'inherited' by a relative of the deceased. For the Bukama *Luo*, this is no new marriage but an extension of the first. It is even possible for the widow to switch among the male relatives if she does not like one or the other. Strictly speaking then, she is not even 'inherited' but simply cared for, even sexually, by the dead person's relatives, who are his surrogates. Any children are the dead man's [he is their *pater* though not their *genitor*]; and since it is not a new marriage, no bridewealth is involved in the (new) union." At the very least, this indicates the complexity of marriage and kinship in Africa, and the danger of easy generalizations, whether anthropological or theological in nature. [Ed.]

[18] Michael C. Kirwen, M.M., *African Widows* (Maryknoll, NY: Orbis Books, 1979), 11.

the sexual act sealing it as in no way sinful. On the contrary, failure or refusal on the part of the man is regarded as invalidating the intended union. The appearance of safari ants in the couple's house at this time is no longer considered to be of any significance.[19]

The practice of a widow wearing pieces of wood (*omind diel*) around her neck, and the cleansing ceremony (*chola*)[20] are slowly dying out. Yet Bukama Catholics maintain that a bereaved woman should not go to the water hole or engage in any kind of hard work for a certain period of time. It seems to me that unconsciously they are still afraid that she might hide the pieces of wood at the water hole, and that these might harm others. But the reason they mention is that this is a way of going to the help of widows in their distress (Jm 1:27) by helping them to perform some of the hard work. Providing a doll for a surviving twin continues, with the explanation that it fulfills the Gospel demand of comforting the suffering.

Because marriageable girls are expected to find a partner and get married as quickly as possible so as to prevent sexual misbehavior, the practices surrounding the burial of such persons continue. Moreover they are defended in the name of observing God's laws and the norms of social decency. Accordingly, Bukama Catholics continue to bury nubile girls who die before marriage outside the village hedge or at the home of their sister's husband. They also continue to perform most of the traditional rituals on other corpses, for the same fundamental reasons. Thus today, no less than in former days, if a pregnant woman dies, the fetus must be separated from its mother's womb before the burial as a mark of religious respect, since two people cannot in normal circumstances be buried in the same grave. These days, however, money rather than a sheep is given to the operator. This suggests to me that the custom remains religiously important in the people's estimation.

Interestingly, during our investigations we determined that the custom of piercing the feet of a deceased barren woman, the performing of the chicken ritual, and the custom of slashing the back of a hunchback, were clearly characterized as disrespectful of the dead. These are no longer being done. However, a widow is still required to be the first to throw soil over her husband's body in the grave, as a sign of her new responsibility as head of the family. But now the palm of the hand is used instead of the elbow as was the case traditionally. The first wife still inherits and sits upon her dead husband's stool or chair. The people explained that a family, just like the church, must

---

[19] See above, under *funerary customs*.

[20] See above, under *funerary customs*.

have a structure and a leader. The ceremony with the *Luo* stool is meant to assure the family of a clear structure of leadership.

Bukama Catholics have discontinued – as being disrespectful of the dead – most of the customs traditionally associated with the death of a leper, a drowned person or a suicide. The practice of burning down the house in which a suicide occurred has been rendered impractical by the type of buildings now constructed: cement blocks and iron sheets have largely replaced the wattle and mud that were universally used previously.

Some Observations

Bukama Catholics never sat down as a community to discuss which of these traditional customs were or were not compatible with their newly ac-quired Catholic beliefs. The synthesis took place spontaneously and, largely, in a practical way. I maintain that the process of synthesis or syncretism was inevitable if the doctrinal, psychological, spiritual and practical differences between *Luo* tradition and Western Christianity were to be resolved. Further, it is my contention that in such situations the integration of popular religiosity is an inevitable and necessary part of the process of inculturation. The crucial question, of course, is whether we can identify the hand of the Holy Spirit in this process – or whether a fragmentation of the Christian community will result. This is the point at issue between the official church and popular religiosity.

How do we understand the processes of syncretism, the development of popular religiosity, and ultimately inculturation itself? These are undoubtedly the most relevant theological questions. In the case of Bukama, at least, it has been a process with aspects we may characterize as *negation* and *affirmation*. On the one hand, the spiritual and religious values of *Luo* traditions are affirmed. On the other hand, one detects a real struggle: the centralization of religious authority and control represented by the official church is in tension with the desire for freedom and self-determination at the local level. Even though not formally articulated as such, the issue is whether the official Catholic perception of death, burial and mourning exhausts the significance of these important moments of human life in the context of the *Luo* worldview.

The syncretistic process we have seen is the Bukama Catholics' answer to this issue. In effect it claims that current official Roman Catholic teaching, though valid in its own way, is not the final word on the subject. Such a Bukama perspective does question the claim of the Catholic Church to be the sole source of religious meaning in Bukama (and by extension, elsewhere). Instead of a singular source of religious meaning, the claim is made for a plurality of sources of more or less equal validity. Yet the current Roman approach is to integrate – or swallow up – all the various streams of religious meaning into one single watercourse, a single river of religious meaning and behavior. As the streams merge, so they lose their individual identity, and so the dual religious consciousness and practice of Bukama Catholics is swept up and swept away. This merging – or submerging – of local traditions and experience is evidence of a deeper process, the significance of which is often lost to all but the very perceptive. South African theologian Takatso A. Mofokeng has seen it, and it concerns human liberation:

> There is, historically, overwhelming evidence that historical Christianity, conservative and progressive, as a Christianity that shares a common history of imposition on the colonized and dominated people, also shares a common intolerance of every indigenous effort at religious creativity. Both wings of colonial Christianity have a hegemonic intolerance of other religions in their conquered spheres of influence. They consequently regard popular religion as a cultural creation of conquered and vanquished people, as a great threat and a challenge to their long established régimes of truth and territorial spheres of influence, and will oppose it as fiercely in the name of orthodoxy and religious uniformity, as the state does in the name of social uniformity, law and order.[21]

This need for liberation in the case of most of Africa is not mechanical or "construed," but lies in the very foundations of the people's religious view of the world. I suppose that is why inculturation is such an intuitive, rather spontaneous process. Sempore refers to this African worldview as "holistic," remarking that it is "characterized by the original conviction that humankind is linked with meta-human beings by working and living together with them."[22] From the moral point of view, I have described it in this way:

> African Religion's conception of morality is steeped in tradition; it flows from God into the ancestors of the people. God is seen as the Great Ancestor, the first Founder and Progenitor, the Giver of Life, the Power behind everything that is. God is the first Initiator of a people's way of life, its tradition. However, the ancestors are the custodians of this tradition. They are its immediate reason for existence and they are its ultimate purpose. The ancestors, who are in constant contact with both God and humanity, often "intrude" into the life of humanity with specific intentions. They do so on their own or through the agency of the spirits. The spirits are active beings who are either disincarnate human persons or powers residing in natural

[21] Takatso Mofokeng, "Popular Religiosity: A Liberative Resource and Terrain of Struggle," in J. van Nieuwenhove and Berma Klein Goldewijk (eds), op. cit., 57.

[22] Sempore, op. cit., 80.

phenomena. [...] Like God and the ancestors, but of lesser power, the spirits also play a part in the moral behavior of human beings. God, the ancestors and the spirits are all powers or forces that impinge on human life in one way or another. In that sense they are all moral agents. The way they act has been determined by the ancestors and is "stored" in the tradition of the people. Tradition, therefore, supplies the moral code and indicates what the people must do to live ethically.[23]

The point here should be clear: it is this worldview, forming the very self-understanding of the people, that has been "imprisoned" by official – or missionary – Christianity. Popular religion is the people's attempt to break free. For this reason, as Sempore notes again, "the existence of popular religion in its Christian and non-christian forms is a fact that imposes itself on us and that we must always discover with interest and sympathy."[24] He warns that religious leaders and theologians should be aware of "the risk of despising and ridiculing the faith of those who live their religion in the depths of life, with few means and little to fall back on."[25] But they should also resist the strong temptation to exploit it for material or whatever personal or institutional advantage, as has undoubtedly often happened. Leaders, he says,

> build shrines and basilicas with looted money in order to lock up the people in factories of devotions. They multiply in abundance the celebrations and objects of worship in order to wrest from the poor the penny of their credulity. They adapt and inculturate pastoral practice in order to control and rule the faithful better. The risk for theology is great and the temptation for the missions is to turn to ideology and tactics. All the more because the weaknesses of popular religion are evident: the illiteracy of the majority prevents them from having direct access to the Scriptures. This makes the believers easy prey for manipulators of the Word.[26]

I cannot resist noting the warning Sempore also gives, in the same place, to the methodical, intellectual and analytic approach to inculturation espoused by official theology (being a member of this group myself). The self-revelation of God is essentially not of a "notional" but an "existential" nature, and so theology "cannot claim any normative character whatsoever" in this realm; like all other "stammerings," it surely cannot lay any (exclusive) claim to orthodoxy. God reveals Godself above all through human existential experience:

---

[23] Laurenti Magesa, *African Religion: The Moral Tradition of Abundant Life* (Maryknoll, NY: Orbis Books, 1997), 35-36.

[24] Sempore, *op. cit.,* 85.

[25] *Ibid.*

[26] *Ibid.*

Popular religion is one of the places, among others, where God reveals Himself to humanity in a process of mutual exodus. It recalls that God is first and foremost a revelation, a being in Exodus, not a brute given, of reason and faith. On the other hand, the life of the relationship between the Africans and their God is characterized by extreme discretion, in strong contrast to the interventionism of the Christian God, the use of liturgies and the multiplication of temples. Does this discretion not come close to the Johannine sobriety of the worship "in spirit and in truth"? Is it certain that the cult of a God who comes out of His silence to proclaim his commandments one by one, to demand submission and to dictate human behavior, means progress for the African religious sensitivity?[27]

Conclusion

Pastoral workers in Africa – clergy, sisters, brothers, catechists – need to understand that inculturation as a process is not a problem for the majority of the people. Most do not understand the fuss about inculturation in its academic form, and frankly they could not care less. But it *does* remain a problem for church officials and for academic theologians, when the spontaneous localization of the Christian faith in popular religiosity is viewed as a distortion of Christian orthodoxy as they understand it. Some officials operate on the understanding that *prescriptive inculturation* promotes more authentic Christianity than *popular inculturation*. What they perhaps overlook is the *sensus fidelium* operating within popular religion, popular religiosity, or the religion of the people: this is a source of vitality for the development of official teaching within the church. The underpinnings – the vernacular forms – are a necessary context into which official universal teachings are translated so as to become meaningful and relevant. As Sempore has explained so graphically:

> Popular religion in Africa is a living and complex reality, which implies the message and its irreducible specificity, the context and its factors of liberation and oppression, and the African people and their desire for salvation. It is a cry which expresses the multiform suffering of a people in search of happiness and liberation; it is a cry calling the messengers of and those responsible for the Word to help; it is the cry of a newly born child in contact with a hard and cruel world, struggling and kicking in the arms of its liberator whom it searches gropingly: the cry of hope.[28]

The future of inculturation seems to me to lie in bridging the gap between the official and popular forms of religious practice: in other words, in further

---

[27] Sempore, *op. cit.,* 86.

[28] Sempore, *op. cit.,* 87.

creative processes of syncretism between the two. Someone has suggested that the way to achieve this is through "communication without domination." Church officials and the masses of the Christian people live in different experiential and conceptual worlds, and so they have different interpretations for experiences as well as different meanings for words, objects and actions. The same religious sign system or language is consequently multivocal. In such a situation, open-ended communication, communication without domination, is essential for the purpose of mutual interrogation and enrichment.

QUESTIONS

1. What is your judgment of the funerary customs that Magesa discusses? Are you as sympathetic toward them, as he is?

2. The *levirate* and *widow inheritance* are clearly important issues for the Christians of Bukama. Yet both these social institutions are complex and difficult for many Western-educated Christians to understand. Undertake some research on the anthropological and theological understandings, and then discuss the *levirate* and *widow inheritance* again, both in the context of Bukama and in other African contexts.

3. Does the author demonstrate his conviction that *prescriptive inculturation* is ineffective? In your opinion, what is its place in the church? What other forms of inculturation does the chapter portray?

4. Recent theological discussion of *syncretism* (referred to as *good syncretism*) has attempted to rehabilitate it within theological discourse. Discuss syncretism in the context of inculturation.

5. Compare Magesa's diagnosis of the cultural health of the *Luo*, with Edwards on the *Tiv*.

CHAPTER SIX

POPULAR PROBLEM-SOLVING
AND INCULTURATION IN DAGBON, GHANA

Jon P. Kirby, S.V.D.

*How can loyal Christians handle some standard cultural issues,
without betraying their faith in Jesus Christ or abandoning their own
social processes of diagnosis and tactical response? How relevant is
the official church to the lives of ordinary Africans? An American
missionary and trained anthropologist ponders these questions from
his experience in Ghana.*

Christian Solutions for African Problems

Popular belief in Ghana holds that Christians have an advantage in
addressing "white man palaver" or problems involving Western institutions:
gaining employment, passing an exam, obtaining medical help or raising a
loan or financial aid. Formerly, when many schools, hospitals and development
projects were run by the churches, this idea might have had some basis, but
it is certainly no longer the case here in *Dagbon* where it is usually more
advantageous politically and economically to be one of the Muslim majority.[1]

A recent research project[2] studied Popular Catholicism[3] among the *Dagomba* of Northern Ghana. It showed that the institutional Roman Catholic
church may be in serious trouble if it continues to focus its ministries on
Western education and medicine, and to encourage people to aspire to Western
cultural forms in a globalized world. Such an approach, which many people
see as only relating to "white man palaver," has not won many *Dagomba*

---

[1] The *Dagomba* are about 45% Muslim. The villages around Tamale average 40% Muslim; remoter
villages are 15-20%. Tamale itself is about 75% Muslim.

[2] A study of popular Catholicism in seven places worldwide, organized by the Maryknoll Fathers
and Brothers and sponsored by the Pew Charitable Trusts, resulted in *Popular Catholicism in a
World Church: Seven Case-studies in Inculturation* (Maryknoll, NY: Orbis Books, 1999). Special
gratitude to Vincent Boi-Nai, S.V.D., project-leader in Tamale, and to the many local people who
assisted him.

[3] *Popular Catholicism* refers to the complex of beliefs and practices (sacramental and devotional,
as well as those related to problem-solving and social change) of 'ordinary' Catholics: those who do
not enjoy much wealth, status, or power. They are the common people. For supportive studies see
Enrique Dussel, "Popular Religion as Oppression and Liberation: Hypothesis on Its Past and
Present in Latin America," *Concilium* 186 (1986), 82-94; and Cristián Parker, *Popular Religion
and Modernization in Latin America: A Different Logic* (Maryknoll, NY: Orbis Books, 1996).

converts: after 50 years less than 2% are Catholic.[4] Nor has it had much effect on the traditional areas of problem-solving in people's everyday lives. "Black man palaver" or African problems, including such typical African religious experiences as witchcraft, "bad death," spirit vengeance, ancestor sanction, and oppression by spirit agencies, are still the major religious problems and the main focus of people's religious problem-solving. Assisting people is one of the most important roles of the church, yet despite its long presence in *Dagbon*, the daily problems of most people remain largely unevangelized. Similar examples can be found across the continent.

Inculturation must begin with local problems. But a first level of understanding must provide an account of the church's historical approach to cultures, and show how it has understood social and religious change. To complement this, we will consider the results of a survey[5] conducted in fifteen villages in the Tamale area of Ghana: this was intended to discover what Christianity means to the people, how they address their problems, and what kind of assistance they feel they need from the church. The approach and methodology for this study followed the general pattern of an earlier study among the *Anufo* of Northern Ghana.[6]

Looking at the church's self-understanding and at how it is perceived by the *Dagomba* people, however, is only part of our concern; we also need a sociological approach to inculturation that will take seriously issues that are problematic for *Dagomba* themselves: every religious problem is context-specific. However, some themes recur across Africa, and so that this chapter will have a wider relevance, we will explore three such issues: divination, "bad death," and witchcraft.

Our survey confirmed that Christianity – particularly Catholicism – is not well-tuned to local problems. Generally, the people felt that the most typically African problems are completely ignored by the official local church. In a moment of frustration, a former voluntary catechist complained bitterly about what he considered a lack of response from the clergy:

> Despite the changes in Africa today, these problems remain with us. Even when we go to our African priests, problems like witchcraft, ancestors and divination are not mentioned because the priests do not take them seriously.

---

[4] P. Barker, *Tribes and Languages of Northern Ghana* (Accra: Evangelism Committee in association with Asempa Publishers, 1986).

[5] The survey was in two parts: part one identified local attitudes to Christianity; part two determined the kinds of religious problems *Dagomba* Christians experience, and how they address them. 45 Muslims, 45 Christians, and 45 Traditionalists were involved.

[6] Jon Kirby, "The Non-Conversion of the *Anufo*," *Mission Studies* IV (1985), 15-25.

Furthermore, we have seen that there is nothing a priest can prescribe to help us to deal with such problems outside of simple prayers and telling us not to believe. Nevertheless we do believe in these things, and we would like the church to help us to make the power of Christ, which we speak of, visible and real.

The religious needs of Africans are indeed real, and as a matter of faith Christians believe that Christ has the power to heal them. But this power is not experienced practically in their everyday lives. Specifically African issues and typical African modes of thinking have been opposed by the Westernized church, so that African Christians tend to keep them hidden: their attitudes are deemed wrong-headed and their worries unreal. But there is another struggle taking place in the lives of many African Christians: in the traditional hierarchy of problem-solving, most of life's daily problems are not considered to fall under the jurisdiction of God but of the lesser spirits and deities. God is far away; taking the problem to God when it ought to be handled by a subordinate, seems presumptuous and disrespectful. The official church seems unaware of this struggle.

Dagomba people do not feel the church is unimportant; they accept it – and science, technology, bio-medicine and other global institutions – even though none of these social facts is fully consonant with African reality or meets all its needs. Western cultural institutions – including the "Mission" churches, and now African local churches – assign different meanings and interpretations to reality than the people do. The fact that this epistemological gap has not yet been bridged by the local church tends to support a parallel approach to problem-solving: Western solutions for "white man palaver" and African solutions for "black man palaver."

Western Cultural Biases

The near-global perspective of scientific materialism now dominates the interpretation of all reality. In respect of their own deeply religious problems, however, Africans experience great inconsistency between their culturally-grounded interpretation of life and the empiricism and pragmatism that pervades the encroaching wave of globalization. Ironically, the church and its formal ministries seem removed from many African problems which are trivialized because they do not fit the scientific, materialistic bias of the modern world.

The process of inculturation is impeded when local church ministers fail to take the spirit world seriously. Bishop Sarpong lamented at the African

Synod that African Bishops had a wrong view of African religion and African life. As evidence of this he cites their

> ample use of such words as polygamy, paganism, heathenism, fetishism, animism, idolatry, and primitive to describe African Traditional Religion ... [These are] not just misnomers, but ... it [is] totally unjust to use such words to describe a reality that in essence is as good as any religious experience. These words, therefore, should be dropped once and for all.[7]

Traditionally, Africans experienced reality as social rather than individual. In Africa today, Christians belong both to their ethnic and to their Christian communities. The two must be harmonized, which is sometimes no easy matter. Christians also need to feel the support of the local church, lest enormous problems arise. An African who maintains he does not believe in witchcraft may still be accused of it, or see his wife murdered or sent to a witch village; or he may suffer misfortunes which others attribute to witchcraft, and thus be drawn back into its vortex of destruction. The Christian community could be of the greatest help here. But the Western bias in favor of individualism may effectively block social action and prevent the leaven of the Gospel from growing in the community. Witchcraft breeds in a social context and needs a social response. As a local prayer leader commented:

> Christians are a minority, and their influence in the local communities is still very small. We Christians would like to protect women accused of witchcraft but we have no way of doing this. If a woman is accused of being a witch, the matter will be taken to the chief and judged there. If she is found guilty she will be sent away to a witch village. We Christians are powerless to interfere. We can only pray that they don't kill the woman and try to encourage our own community to help wherever we can.

Western biases towards materialism and individualism, perpetuated by the forces of globalization, widen the gap between African traditional religious explanations of reality and scientific dogma. The official church often fails to bridge the gap; yet it is being slowly bridged at unofficial or local levels in *Dagbon,* where "popular Catholicism" is the norm.[8]

Toward a New Identity in Dagbon

When the British arrived in Northern Ghana a century ago, they found chiefs and traditional states in only four tribes: *Gonja, Mamprusi, Wala* and

---

[7] Peter Sarpong, "Conclusion," in Maura Browne (ed.), *The African Synod: Documents, Reflections, Perspectives* (Maryknoll, NY: Orbis Books, 1996), 223.

[8] The traditional Kingdom of the *Dagomba* people presently covers about 10,000 sq. km in Northern Ghana.

Dagomba.[9] Through their policy of *indirect rule* the British solved the problem of governing the forty or so "chiefless" tribes by putting them under the authority of tribes with chiefs, especially the *Dagomba.*

A long slave-raiding tradition did not dispose the *Dagomba* to rule these politically minor tribes democratically. Since Independence, the reins of political power have remained in the hands of the *Dagomba* and the other chiefly groups. The sons of chiefs have become the lawyers and politicians of the North. As the focal point of Northern politics moved from control over people to control over land in the late 1970s, these "chiefly" politicians sought and obtained rights in land through the Constitutions of 1979, whereby all Northern Region lands came under the jurisdiction of the traditional chiefs. Since then, the North has witnessed a series of conflicts that have strongly polarized the two political groupings of "chiefly" and "non-chiefly" peoples. In 1994 a massive "Northern Conflict" led to the loss of 20,000 lives; hundreds of thousands were made homeless.[10]

Great losses and even greater humiliation were suffered among the *Dagomba,* producing social *anomie.* Now their faith in institutionalized chieftaincy (*naam*) and their right to rule the "minor" tribes is being questioned for the first time, and they are even beginning to question their old relationship to God (*Naawuni*), the very deification of chiefly hierarchy. To a people who have always associated victory with God's favor, defeat raises the disturbing question whether the God of their enemies is more powerful and more "true."

Anomie creates a vacuum that is being filled by militant Islam introduced by Muslim missionaries, but there is also an increasing interest in Christianity. However, Islamic fundamentalism is rapidly replacing the old *laissez faire* attitude toward other religions,[11] and the current openness is likely to subside if Christ does not soon become more recognizable as a *Dagomba.*

There is an explicit religious and political dimension to the identity crisis. Early on, Christianity had made great progress with some of the chiefless "minority" tribes, which have produced all of the current northern bishops and most of the local clergy. Thus, in popular thinking, Christianity is associated

[9] J. D. Fage, "Reflections on the Early History of the Mossi-Dagomba Group of States," in J. Vansina, R. Mauny, and L. V. Thomas (eds), *The Historian in Tropical Africa* (London: Oxford University Press, 1964); M. Staniland, *The Lions of Dagbon: Political Change in Northern Ghana* (Cambridge: Cambridge University Press, 1975); E. F. Tamakloe, *A Brief History of the Dagomba People* (Accra: Government Printers, 1931); I. Wilks, *The Northern Factor in Ashanti History* (Legon: Institute of African Studies, University of Ghana, 1961).

[10] J. Katanga, "Stereotypes and the Road to Reconciliation in Northern Ghana," *Uhuru* 6, 9 (1994), 19-22.

[11] P. Barker, *op. cit.*

with them. Conversely, the church was unsuccessful with the "chiefly" peoples who usually preferred the old order to change. The association of Muslim clerics with the traditional states, and their adoption of the Islamic calendar, dress, and customs, all predisposed the chiefly peoples more toward Islam.[12] As the education level of the "minorities" increased through mission schools, so their dissent grew. Many *Dagomba* leaders now blame the church for the current discord.

The ethnic conflicts caught the attention of the world and led to some political gains for the minority tribes; but such conflicts do not bring about a new order. At best they reproduce the same inequalities with different figure-heads. Injustice in land tenure policies, in the ethnic division of power, and in the continued use of such concepts as *slave* and *master* can only be overcome from within the local communities.

This then is the broad historical context in which small Christian Communities or CCs[13] are effectively *Dagomba*-izing Christ and the church.

Village-level Transformations

At the time of the conflict and in its aftermath, the Catholic church was accused by some *Dagomba* people of aligning itself with the "minorities". Part of the hostility was due to earlier criticism by the church[14] of the "feudalistic" practices of the state systems; but much was due to the propaganda of Muslim fundamentalists. In this situation the CCs succeeded in calming the community by demonstrating the even-handedness of the official church, especially through their community-based work in adult education, literacy classes and small development projects which were designed to benefit everyone. The Christian Communities are also demonstrating new styles of leadership, emphasizing love and service and urging a more equitable basis for sharing common resources. The power of the CCs caught the attention of the local church, and since then the interest and activities of the broader church have increased.

---

[12] N. Levitzon, *Muslims and Chiefs in West Africa: A Study of Islam in the Middle Volta Basin in the Pre-Colonial Period* (Oxford: Clarendon Press, 1968); I. Wilks, "A Note on the Early Spread of Islam in Dagomba," *Transactions of the Historical Society of Ghana* 8 (1965).

[13] Each village we studied has a leader and a small group of Catholics – which we refer to here as "Christian Communities" – who pray together and celebrate liturgical and social occasions in common.

[14] See Peter K. Sarpong (ed.), *Inter-Tribal Conflicts in Ghana* [*Catholic Bishops' Conference of Ghana: Justice and Peace Commission*], (Kumasi: Cita Press, 1984).

100

Catholics of *Dagbon* are demonstrating a new way of living that involves a special kind of love that is needed for these times. But they are doing it as *Dagomba*. They gather every morning and evening for prayers, singing, instruction – and sometimes literacy classes – as their Muslim neighbors go to the mosque for prayer. The relationship with Muslims, beginning with members of their own families, is a true dialogue. The people are not isolated from their neighbors, and one can almost feel the growth of a new *Dagomba* identity as these communities come together for prayer, initiate local development, and restructure family life – while living as Christ's church contextualized within a *Dagomba* village. Husbands marry only one wife and stay with her even if she is barren. We cannot fully grasp the symbolism of the church as "bride of Christ" in *Dagbon* until there are more *Dagomba* Christian wives. Currently the number of Catholic women is less than half that of the men, yet they are already exerting a great influence, as seen by their involvement in health-and-hygiene education and in small-scale development projects: cloth-weaving, soap-making, tree-planting and shea-nut-processing. Women are encouraged by their husbands to go to night classes, and to learn new productive skills which contribute to the needs of the family.

All these activities generate transformative power in the local community. The church, too, takes more notice and offers more assistance: more help in literacy-training, liturgical translation, and specifically women's projects. Yet much remains to be done. With more Religious sisters in their midst, and with increased sponsorship of women's community development projects, women's voices could be amplified. The church, both "popular" and "official," local and universal, could collaborate still more intentionally and effectively.

Muslim influence has increased enormously over the past couple of decades. In Tamale it is sometimes said that "the *Dagomba* should all be Muslims." *Dagomba* Christians are sometimes told they "don't respect" and are "traitors to their own culture and traditions." But the *Dagomba* crave respect as much as food or life itself. Interestingly then, our survey revealed that most *Dagomba* are willing to acknowledge that Christians do respect *Dagomba* traditions, chiefs and elders, and the *Dagomba* way of life. Many even commented that Christians, unlike Muslims, love everyone, not just fellow-Christians. Thus *Dagomba* Christians are perceived differently in the villages where they live alongside their own people – kin and neighbors – than in the anonymity of a Muslim-dominated city.

Dagomba Christians strongly affirm everything about their traditions except what goes against church teaching. But what really is "church teaching" in the context of *Dagomba* daily life? Since very little has been researched, the church cannot say much about family life or traditional institutions such as marriage, funerals, name-giving ceremonies or other rites of passage. Yet by keeping the traditions of giving and receiving respect, the CCs are at least affirming the importance of traditional cultural values as the basis for new *Dagomba* Christian values. By re-shaping these values and traditions such as respect for chieftaincy (*naam*) in the image of Christ, especially "Christ the King," they are leading the way in the process of inculturation and offering new directions in ministry for the local church.

The village-level activities of the CCs are truly initiatives in inculturation. Despite failings, people are living out the Gospel in local situations through loving service; despite limitations, they are doing their best to mold their understanding of church teaching to their real needs and daily problems, whether "African" or "Western"; despite occasional conflicts, their relations with Muslims are peaceful. At the heart of the dialogue is a common religious heritage of traditional *Dagomba* religious beliefs and practices, especially those that address problems like bad dreams, children crying in the night, occasions when divination is indicated, and the need to call on ancestors.

The CCs yearn for Christian solutions to *Dagomba* problems. They need prayer rituals for situations which normally call for traditional prayer: in times of illness, when building a house, at times of planting or harvest. Here especially, help from the official church is warranted. Only in the mutual interaction of the popular and the official church can the people of God hope to arrive at lasting solutions. But the church must first enter more deeply into the religious life of the people. It must begin to bridge the cultural and interpretative gap.

Being Dagomba and Christian

Dagomba Catholics are a source of attraction and puzzlement to their neighbors: their Christianity is at odds with their *Dagomba* identity with its roots in traditional beliefs liberally laced with Islamic customs; they are not the typical warlike *Dagomba* who became the most politically powerful tribe in the north; nor, from the perspective of the official Roman Catholic church, are they model Christians. One of the local pastors described them as "a weak lot" – explaining that at times they seem to lack commitment. Nevertheless, in some ways their faith is quite surprising. Perhaps the most remarkable outcome of the survey was that their fellow villagers couldn't help but notice that "they love one another" and "they pray."

It is most unusual for *Dagomba* people to love one another without a good utilitarian motive; and while Muslims pray, they do so to obtain merit (*lada*), which becomes an antidote for dealing with whatever difficulty they are experiencing. *Dagomba* enjoy power politics. They know that access to God brings power, as their many Islamic amulets and Qur'anic verses, used magically, testify. The Christians, however, do not try to control God. In typical African fashion, the *Dagomba* put the matter into God's hands as a last resort. But for the Christians this is no longer a fatalistic exercise. To them it is an assent in faith and hope that God will respond with an overabundance of power to meet their needs – in God's own good time. Non-Christian *Dagomba* seem to be watching and waiting to see if this power materializes.

For the most part, *Dagomba* Catholics and their neighbors still see the power of God most clearly demonstrated in material success and prosperity. The official church has done impressively well to Christianize this view. But people do need help with their "African problems." Although traditionally this was the domain of various deities and lesser spirits, Christianity avers that the God of Jesus is jealous of our prayer, and wishes us to come to Him with all our problems: He is the Lord of all. The official church needs to break through the boundaries of African Religion so that God's Lordship can be exercised here as well.

When people were asked why they have become Catholic, three main reasons were given: *truth, heaven,* and *forgiveness.* All three topics resonate with and address *Dagomba* concerns. *Truth* is desired because it represents integration – living in a way that blends *Dagomba* traditions with Gospel values and church teaching. *Truth* has already been indicated through the traditions established by the ancestors and is embodied in their customs – particularly those practices that have been affected by Islam and chieftaincy – even if these are the most suspect to the official church. *Heaven* refers to life after death, but also to the hope of God's kingdom on earth, a tangible experience of God's power and glory among the living. *Forgiveness* means that one puts faith in the unconditional love of God, cultivating an attitude of dependence on God rather than conquest of other people as in times past. One admits guilt and seeks pardon. All three themes affirm and build on *Dagomba* tradition, yet indicate the yearning for a new revelation of God's power, to be discovered not in the triumphalism of the past but in service, not in ethnic militancy or conflict but through a love that overrides even the desire for life itself. *Truth, heaven* and *forgiveness* lead to new life underpinned by the Holy Spirit; the fruit of the Spirit is the new kingdom glimmering faintly in the midst of the CCs. These are the foundations of *Dagomba* Christian identity and spirituality. They must be nurtured by the official church.

Becoming a Christian can be difficult, for it excludes converts from full participation in *Dagomba* society, yet leaves them with no practical ways of addressing traditional problems. Despite Christianity's attraction, *Dagomba* elders ask: "Can one learn to pray like a Christian and still truly be a

Dagomba?" Many find it impossible to forego their traditional and Muslim-influenced customs or the support of their communities, families and friends. That would be to deny their identity. They find they can't really live a life separate from their own people.

A few church leaders ask why this should be necessary. Should not the local church help the people feel more at home in their communities as both *Dagomba* and Christian? The church has officially espoused this approach in Pope Paul VI's *Evangelii Nuntiandi* in 1975; it was reconfirmed at the African Synod in 1996; and theologians[15] have strongly indicated that the only solid base for a vibrant local Christianity is its rooting in the local ethnicity and culture. Nor is this something new for the church: Jesus reproved his disciples, saying, "... not one dot, not one little stroke, shall disappear from the law until its purpose is achieved" (Mt 5:17-19). In Africa, ancestors and other unseen agents of the "kingdom" embody the traditional law; and despite repeated attempts by the church to remove them, they remain a reproof to the church by resisting until their purpose is achieved in the African economy of salvation.

The Need for Christian Problem-solving Rituals

In the limited ways now available to them (through simple prayer services and by blending their traditions as best they can with Christian love and prayer), the CCs are already committed to inculturation. The official church must also be committed, coming to understand the problems of the people – particularly the typically African problems – and assisting them with direction, support and rituals. In the past, the official church has dictated how and where Christians must direct their religious behavior: not toward *juju* or "primitive" notions like witchcraft. If the church is to be relevant to the life-experience of the people, it must engage more appropriately with the local communities and help people build a new sacramental life based on their own worldview. The problem-solving and ritual approaches of the Muslims have something to teach the Christian church in Africa.

The *Dagomba* recognize more than fifty problems[16] which need special attention and ritual responses. The latter involve spirits, divination, shrines and sacrifices (offerings). "Bad death" and "witchcraft" are among the most

---

[15] Stephen B. Bevans, *Models Of Contextual Theology* (Maryknoll, NY: Orbis Books, 1992); Aylward Shorter, *Toward a Theology of Inculturation* (London: Geoffrey Chapman, 1988); Robert J. Schreiter, *Constructing Local Theologies* (Maryknoll, NY: Orbis Books, 1985).

[16] These include divination, sacrifices and libations, "bad death," ancestor sanctions, incest, oaths, lightning strikes, barrenness, witchcraft, taboos, birth defects, widowhood, bad luck, twin prob-

serious; both reflect African understandings of causality and of good and evil. The following section offers an ethnographic account, a theological reflection, and a suggested pastoral approach.

A. *Divination: Discovering the Cause of a Problem*

Description

Although people understand the natural or immediate causation of various problems, misfortunes or illnesses, elders inquire after the final cause and the personal connection. It is not sufficient to identify *how* the problem occurred: *who* is ultimately responsible must be discovered. A critical question is: why this person, and not someone else? Divination reveals the links between the material world and the unseen world, helping elders interpret events and seek solutions. Through offerings, libations and invocations, by prayers and sacrifices directed to the ancestors, spirits, and the Supreme Being, things can he made right again.

Dagomba diviners, like the Hebrew prophets, do not so much tell the future as the past and the present. Their art is meant to reveal the true state of one's relationship to the unseen world. Misfortunes are indications of trouble in this domain. The symbolic patternings of divination are the "vital signs" of this relationship. Although the components of the diagnosis are neutral in themselves (house, woman, child, ancestors, twins), clients would expect the cause of the problem to be some imbalance in normal relationships. Thus, the diagnosis may indicate house problems, woman palaver, child's illness, ancestor sanction, or the malicious behavior of a twin spirit. Once the problem is diagnosed, elders and specialists can begin re-harmonizing relationships through the appropriate sacrifices and rituals.

Among the *Anufo*, another Islamized society of Northern Ghana, Islam has succeeded in redirecting traditional causal thinking by offering new interpretations of the symbols and rites of divination.[17] Their form of divination allows God to penetrate their problem-solving processes, offering greater hope and security for all. It offers hope because of an emphasis on the positive: when a Muslim diviner discloses the signs that a traditionalist would interpret as the presence of witchcraft, he interprets them in a positive way – for example,

---

lems, death, childbirth, naming, house building, first fruits, oracles, magic, madness, bad dreams and many others.

[17] Jon Kirby, "The Anthropology of Knowledge and the Christian Dialogue with African Traditional Religions," *Missiology* 3 (1992), 323-341.

as only a *potential* threat, which can be prevented by God's power over the *lesser* spirits. It offers security, because the Islamic influence assures God's powerful help through prayer and ritual, the pillars of Islam, and in the many amulets and other protective devices derived from the Qur'an. Hope and a sense of security lead to a future orientation and a preventative mentality, because only then is there freedom to look beyond a current crisis.

Theological Reflections

In the Torah (Ex 20:3-6; Dt 5:7-10), exclusive loyalty to the "One Living and True God" is mandated. The same is demanded in the New Testament (Lk 4:8; Mk 12:24-30; 1 Cor 8:6, 10:6-9). The use of (African) divination, rituals and sacrifices might seem incompatible with these injunctions, and African Protestant leaders and missionaries are very clear about this. One involved in Bible translation among the *Dagomba* speaks for many:

> Christians must not go to diviners. The book of Exodus gives us clear direction here ... Christianity offers a new way of living without depending on idols and false gods. We have only one God who is our savior, Jesus Christ. The old way needs divination and diviners to deal with its problems but Christians do not need such things.

The Old Testament considered consultation of the spirit world through divination and spirit mediumship to be aberrations (Dt 18:10-12; 1 Sam 28:3-9; Lev 19:31, 20:6, 27; 2 Kgs 21:6). But we should distinguish the therapeutic need to seek direction and assurances in misfortune, from the kinds of direction and assurances that are given. Nothing in God's law condemns the search for meaning in an unfortunate situation. Indeed, this was the primary role of the prophets in the Old Testament, and it is the basis of Christian ministry in our time. The human need to be concerned with final causes and deeper meanings is a God-given inclination. What is unacceptable is the projection of wrongful, inappropriate and inaccurate meanings and interpretations, especially those that stifle creative and loving human responses.

The *Dagomba* know that God is more powerful than all spirits; but only Muslims offer a way to enlist God's help for their problems. Christians hold that God's love overcomes all; but they also need to hear and experience this in their daily lives. They need to know that misfortunes are not simply signs of God's disfavor and that they can count on God's love and help, through prayer rather than blood sacrifice. A contrite heart and a spirit of self-sacrifice are pleasing to God. The people must hear and see this in concrete ways.

Christian Ritual and Pastoral Implications

Our survey showed that Christians and non-Christians alike consult diviners as they have always done. The church's ministers are aware of it. One local priest acknowledges: "Sooth-saying is a big problem, but we are only now starting to address it by becoming more involved in people's problems. In the past we presumed that the converts knew they shouldn't go to the diviners: that it was against Christianity. I guess we presumed too much."

But even new attempts at involvement are insufficient unless they take traditional problems seriously, and offer Christian solutions that respond to the contexts of village life. One of our prayer leaders said: "We Christians do not go to priests with such problems. We are going to diviners. We can't help it. We have no choice. We are living among pagans. It is our way of life. Even the Muslims go to diviners. They have their own diviners who help them in the Muslim way. We would like it if priests were more like diviners, taking a more active role in solving our traditional problems." African traditional religions do not separate the material and spiritual worlds; Christianity could make a better job of integrating life.

The survey showed that many people – traditionalists and Muslims – believe that Christians do have their own (albeit unofficial) solutions to *Dagomba* problems. Some Christians believe that official Christian solutions should exist for these problems; most responded that the Christian solution is prayer. Yet most people revert to traditional means if problems persist. A prayer leader expressed his concerns like this: "We Christians have the one way, the true way, but the Muslims have solutions to many of our traditional problems which the church does not have. People would all like it if we too have solutions." Such hopes are not generally shared by the clergy. Many priests interpret such needs as a sign of weakness: "They go to diviners because they want immediate results. Those whose faith is mature are different. They do not need such solutions." One priest said he felt that the church needs to be stricter and that the Assemblies of God are exemplary here, because they "do not compromise their principles."

The issue of immediate results was often raised by clergy (but not the people generally) as the main reason for the popularity of diviners. But this betrays a basic misunderstanding of divination, for diviners do not provide immediate results.[18] Their prescriptions must be validated by trial and error. Dismissing people's problems with statements like "they do not need such

---

[18] Jon Kirby, *loc. cit.*

solutions" betrays cultural obtuseness. The fact is, people do have these needs and they should not be left to find their own solutions to religious problems, any more than to health or food problems. The church's obligation is to help incarnate Christ, to make the power of Christ visible and real. The advice given by Muslim diviners is an excellent example of good counsel that could be given by Christian diviner/priests.

The crucial difference between a traditional diviner and a diviner/priest is more basic than a desire for results or solutions. It is in the focus of these solutions. Traditional diviners tend to dredge up and affirm people's most basic instincts, or confirm their worst fears and suspicions. A good pastor raises a person's eyes beyond such concerns. Muslim diviners can reduce negative influences and emphasize the positive by continually referring to the presence of God's power and direction during the divination, through statements like "God is there!"; "We want white and not black things!"; "We want white teeth, happiness!"; "Long life and prosperity are with God!"; "By prayer you will get what you need!"[19]

Ethnographic research[20] into divination among the *Anufo* can help Christian ministers to distinguish between various symbols of divination and their interpretation. Rather than going to a traditional diviner, troubled Christians could consult a Christian healer or priest/diviner with a charism for the discernment of spirits, who understands people's thinking and their need for counseling as prescribed in 1 Cor 12:4-11. In the absence of a priest/diviner, the Christian community, through common prayer, becomes the living presence of Christ and the proper source of such discernment. Here in *Dagbon* some priests are already acting as priest/diviners when they direct the faithful to appropriate prayer, ritual and action in the light the gospel sheds on their traditional problems. We need more such involvement.

B. Bad Death: Working within the Dagomba Worldview

Description

Across Africa certain types of death are so polluting that in themselves they prevent any possibility of continuance, of fulfilling one's destiny, of becoming an ancestor. In *Dagbon* they include death in childbirth, death by drowning, ,

---

[19] Jon Kirby, "The Islamic Dialogue with African Traditional Religion: Divination and Health Care," in *Social Science and Medicine* 36 (1993), 237-249.

[20] Jon Kirby, *God, Shrines and Problem-solving among the Anufo of Northern Ghana* (Collectanea Instituti Anthropos 35. Sankt Augustin: Anthropos Institute, 1986).

suicide, death in an epileptic fit, death by lightning, or dying alone with no one to put water in one's mouth. In some cases, like drowning, a special purification rite is made before the funeral; in others, as death in childbirth or death alone in the bush, no funerary rites are prescribed but the purification rites serve as a "non-funeral." The victims of such "bad deaths" cannot become ancestors, their names are never again repeated, and they cease to exist in social consciousness.

If the person dies in a room, the corpse cannot be taken out through the doorway lest it somehow find its way back in to human commerce; so a hole is knocked in the wall to remove it. The body is unceremoniously dragged to the bush where it is "thrown" into a shallow grave hemmed about by powerful medicines that are believed to incarcerate the wayward spirit, preventing it from harming the local people. The possessions of the deceased are so polluted that they can only be claimed by a very powerful medicine man who has been called upon to perform the various rites. Body and soul are cut off from human contact and it becomes a fearsome "thing of the bush." After the corpse is disposed of, the house must be cleansed with the sacrifice of a sheep (an Islamic influence) and its blood must be sprinkled about the whole compound. Finally the compound is again doused, this time with purifying medicinal water that has been steeped in special roots, bark and leaves; and a diviner is consulted to verify the cause of the abominable death.

Fear of bad death leads to many inhuman practices. A woman experiencing a difficult delivery will be harangued by the midwives to tell the name of a presumed secret lover; if it appears she may die, her child is pulled from her womb along with the placenta and uterus, thus killing her and often the child as well. But, as they say, "at least it is not bad death."

Bad death is not only abominable in itself but is a threat to the social life of the community. If all women were to die in childbirth, if all lives were to be cut short in suicide or by natural disasters like lightning, society itself would soon cease to exist. The event is interpreted as the chaos of the "bush" intruding into the human life-cycle. Traditional rituals governing the handling of the corpse are the means of controlling this anomaly. Purification rites redefine the boundaries of the bush and society. The culprit is named as a "spirit of the bush" and is unceremoniously returned to the bush whence it came. The human name is struck from social memory. Never again will this chaotic incarnation repeat itself. The visible boundaries are strengthened as the corpse is hemmed about with magical medicines. Boundary-making extends to the unseen world as well. The company of the ancestors in the "afterlife/beforelife" has been violated by divisive elements in the unseen world, "spirits of the bush" seeking to destroy society from within through untimely death, disorder and destruction. Behind this explanation lies a cosmology uniting the world of the seen and the unseen, the living and the dead. When a child enters the world of the living from its resting place with the ancestors to be nominally re-incarnated as one who has gone before, it proclaims its purpose before God, thus setting its destiny. In the course of life's events, if such an abominable death overtakes a person, it is seen as a result of this destiny. It is thus a betrayal, the manifestation of an impostor, for no real ancestor would wantonly cause such a catastrophe. To *Dagomba* it is the malicious prank of a destructive, chaotic spirit, and serious measures must be taken to isolate the impersonator and limit the harm caused.

Theological Reflections

Christians give new meaning and dignity to life and death; no death is so abominable that it lessens this dignity. In the view of Christians death is only a temporary separation of the soul from the body. The matter of the body returns to the earth until the day of the resurrection of the dead and the soul returns to God. Some criteria of "bad death" are contested by Christians on theological grounds. Deaths that are marked as anti-social because the person died alone in the bush, by drowning, or by suicide, rather than surrounded by family and loved ones are not polluting. Christians believe that no one ever dies alone; God is always present. Only the death of one's spirit is abhorrent. So Christians bury their dead with the dignity that befits a "temple of the Holy Spirit" (1 Cor 10:4 and Dt 21:23). Jesus died a shameful death, indeed a "bad death" (Col 3:14), and Romans later mocked it by drawing him on a cross with the head of an ass. But we believe that it was through Christ's death that we were redeemed from the curse of sin and fear. Through the "bad death" of Jesus, all deaths were made good.

For inculturation and ritual purposes, Christians must determine how death is truly good news and good for them. How can the new meaning and dignity of death be demonstrated within the traditional cosmology? In the case of *Dagomba* and of other African peoples, the traditional means for dealing with "bad death," however severe, are quite limited. They contain the evil but do not vanquish it, and not every evil is included. But in the death of Jesus, all death has been overcome once and for all. So the Christian conquest of all evil is indeed "good news" that should be celebrated ritually. In *Dagomba* cosmology, life is a continuum, a cyclic track through the realms of the living and the dead. Death and birth are the meeting points. Here the seen and unseen worlds unite. Our links with the ancestors and with each other, and our destiny before God, are core elements of a cosmology that can be made to blossom with new meaning and dignity – all of which might be ritually celebrated.

Christian Ritual and Pastoral Implications

Muslim mortuary rites appeal to all *Dagomba* people. They bury their "bad death" victims with a full funeral, and people believe the power of their prayers (*adu'a*) controls the contagion and reduces the effects of the evil. But Christians, too, could propose their own rituals in such cases, and explain and demonstrate through the symbols of the rite how the powers of evil are vanquished. Traditionalists and Muslims, as well as other Christians, would all be grateful.

An initial step in restructuring Christian *Dagomba* funeral rites for infants has already been taken. This too has been inspired by the rites of the Muslims. Traditionally, infants are given burial rites or a "first funeral," but are not made ancestors through the extended mortuary rites called "second funeral." A local leader said: "We Christians are changing our custom with the new rites of 'second funeral' for infants and small children. Traditionalists do not do anything special for them but the Muslims do and now we Christians do as well, so that everyone knows that even infants are children of God." The rituals are not only for the Christian community but bring greater understanding, dignity and life to the entire community. They assure the community that God has power over all evils including death.

New rites must also be prepared for bad death victims. Ministers must be eliminate dehumanizing practices in the treatment of corpses, widows, widowers or family members. Each step of the Christian funeral should overtly express God's presence and power over death. Scriptural readings and prayers addressing the fearful anti-social nature of the death and the fact that the person is specially blessed by the imitation of Jesus' own death could be a part of this. The priest and the Christian community must be supportively present in this time of bereavement. They may also be called upon to perform various secular and ritual functions, such as bathing and anointing the corpse, in place of the traditional specialists. The family and the household should be blessed with holy water and prayed over. Some time after all the mortuary rites have been performed, a final ceremony accompanied by readings from the psalms and a short homily of encouragement might take place, during which everything and everyone might once again be purified by holy water.

C. Witchcraft and Sorcery: The Problem of Evil

Description

Witches are believed to be people who work in concert with evil forces or who have magical powers within themselves to bring about evil, selfish, individualistic ends. In *Dagbon,* witchcraft is both a spiritual and physical force. It is morally reprehensible, for witches must choose to practice their activities, which always end in death. Witches are believed able to transform themselves at will into wild animals, black cats, snakes, birds of prey and horses; they can choose to kill by invisible means such as slowly sucking the life from their victims; or they can work through natural means such as poisons or even car accidents. They are believed to sit together at night on desolate escarpments or tree-tops, as red lights visible to passers-by. They chat, attract new members and plan new destructive activities against humankind in general but particularly against their own family members. In *Dagbon,* social harmony is cherished, and disruption – especially from inside one's own extended family – is utterly unacceptable. The family heads are ever-vigilant against such friction, which is a sure sign of witchcraft. It is universally believed to be a root cause of evil, and advice and protection are regularly sought through divination and oracles. The worst evil, the most dangerous source of disharmony, involves the perversion of society's norms regarding status.

Witches can be of either gender but are usually thought of as being troublesome old women. Social neuroses within *Dagomba* society tend to produce an abnormal number of such women. Indeed, "old woman" is a euphemism for witch. A woman's security rests almost totally on the strength and support of her son. This occasions many tensions and conflicts. When the child is small, the focus of the rivalry is between a woman and her co-wives, each of whom is promoting her own sons. Later, tensions arise between her and her son's wife or wives, who are each competing for the man's limited attention and resources. In such situations, suspicion and envy – the seeds of witchcraft accusation – take root. A woman with no son, or one who is weak or unstable, is virtually defenseless. If she and her son are strong, his wife may end up accused as the witch.

In the past and even now, wives are taken from the former slave minorities and low status commoners. Any status women have is acquired through their menfolk. A man can rise in status through his father, but just as slaves and commoners are subject to the ruling classes, so a woman is always a "slave" to her husband and son. The system breeds acute competition and tension. Tension and insecurity have been increased by changing economic conditions, which also involve women.

Dagomba women are a prestige symbol for their men. They are put on a pedestal and they do not work on the farms as do the women of the surrounding "minority" groups,[21] yet the men have to work harder now than they ever did in the past when they raided or extorted the surrounding peoples. Now the men are under greater economic pressure and stress, for they cannot fulfill their role as providers. Development initiatives of late have favored the women, but results have not always been positive. Women can easily earn more than their husbands, but they often stockpile their earnings into capital goods that fall into the category of "women's things" like cloth and enamel cookware, which become the only instance of personal property within an otherwise communal society. A woman is under no obligation to give these resources to anyone, and it would bring shame on a man if he were to ask or even accept help from his wife for such necessities as food, medical care, clothing or children's school fees. If a man cannot manage his responsibilities it is grounds for divorce. Tensions are rising even higher and witchcraft accusations abound.

Within *Dagomba* society, higher status only brings greater security if there is enough grass roots support. The striving for status and security is highly competitive and can result in further conflict which, in turn, can produce witchcraft accusations. Accusations act as a leveling device, reinforcing hierarchies and limiting access to power. They also demonstrate the power of the common people in maintaining the system. Nowadays higher status can be gained through a variety of means, especially education and development. Though Christians have greater access to these means, they are also at greater risk. Since they are few in number, and have little authority locally, they must rely heavily on the support of the official church, which, as we saw, is viewed by some as a betrayal. On another level, we find a parallel in the competition for status between *Dagomba* and the "minority" tribes. Here too Christians have come to be associated with those who try to bypass the rules for gaining status.

Formerly, persons declared to be witches were stoned or beaten to death by the community. Not only during the colonial era but since Independence, too, women have been consigned to "witch villages," the chiefs of which are believed to have special powers to control them. People who dared take the law into their own hands by stoning a putative witch were hanged. The problem itself has not abated over the years; the number of accusations seems

---

[21] David Tait, "A Sorcery Hunt in Dagomba," *Africa* 33 (1963), 136-147.

to have increased. But nowadays the law has lost its grip; the youth frequently take matters into their own hands and kill the accused.

Theological Reflections

Dagomba Catholics strongly believe in witchcraft. One of the prayer leaders had this to say: "Witchcraft is a fact. Women accused of witchcraft have been 'promising' to the earth shrines (*bugri*). We have seen them doing it. We have caught them in the act." Another said: "I believe in witchcraft but as a Christian I don't believe that it can harm me." Still another demonstrated that the mentality of *Dagomba* Christians is not far from that of their non-Christian brothers and sisters who are helplessly caught up in it: "Even the Christians are involved in witchcraft accusations. Recently the Christian community in one of our villages went to the chief and accused a woman of witchcraft. They wished to have her removed from the village." And one can sense the hopelessness in this comment by a village leader: "We have a proverb that goes: 'Women are like dogs: if you declare a dog mad and kill it, the dog has no choice but to accept it.' It is the same with women accused of witchcraft. If they declare your wife a witch, that's all. She is finished!"

These days Christians are frequently the targets of witchcraft accusations, so there is an urgent need for a practical pastoral response, which can only be based on a theological analysis. The following case was offered by one of the leaders: "A Christian woman who had been suspected of witchcraft visited her brother in *Kumbuyili*. During the visit the son of her brother got sick and was sent to the [medical] doctor. Then the woman went back to her village. The boy died and the woman was accused in her absence. The people said they would have killed her if she had been around. What does the church say about the woman?" The pastoral problem in itself is complex and fraught with danger, for Christians are a minority. The local pastor warned: "We must find a way of supporting women accused of witchcraft! But we are so few. What power can we exert? If one of us is accused of witchcraft, what can we say or do to change it?" Christians stand out as entrepreneurs and innovators, which now makes even the young men susceptible to accusation. When accusations are supported by the chiefs, the counterbalance of church support must be very strong indeed.

Here is the prayer-leader of a Christian Community: "Recently a young man died in a lorry accident, and when they went to diviners to find out the cause they discovered it was due to one of the young men of the village, a Catholic boy. He was publicly accused of witchcraft and driven out of his village. In protest the case was taken all the way to the Tamale chief, but he too supported the witchcraft accusation. What is to be the role of Christians in such unjust accusations? If you are accused, there is nothing you can do to prove your innocence."

Witches are seen as the very personification of evil. But those accused are mere pawns, not the ultimate causes. The pattern of accusations and convictions is built into society as a whole. Yet often the various means used to dispense with the evil – murder, incarceration or banishment without trial – bring greater harm to the victims and the perpetrators in a never-ending cycle of jealousy, suspicion and hatred. In the end, society itself is victimized and rendered helpless. It is social sin in its most deadly form, and exorcising the demon requires more than simply rituals, though they too are necessary; it requires the application of social justice to all forms of subjugation and coercion.

Christian Ritual and Pastoral Implications

There are two pastoral issues here: the politics of witchcraft with its implications for social justice, and the need to mend the lives of those personally affected. The church's ministry must, therefore, be multi-faceted; it is not enough for the church simply to preach against the treatment of those accused. Accusers and accused must be ministered to, and wounds must be salved. Both the immediate and the deeper causes must be addressed. The situations that occasion witchcraft accusations – like senseless deaths and epidemics – need special attention; and the deeper social issues – like injustice, inequalities and subjugation – must be set right. The laws of the nation must be enforced. Youth must not commit murder with impunity. Here the official church has great power and must use it.

We have characterized witchcraft as a leveling device and a by-product of tensions produced in the competition for status that is inherent in *Dagomba* chieftaincy (*naam*). Only a transformation at the heart of *Dagomba* society and the *naam* can fully handle this problem. Christians cannot bring this about unless they are perceived as being thoroughly *Dagomba*, and unless they have popular support.

A study of *Dagomba* witchcraft[22] makes it clear that although the Muslims feature prominently in the drama of witchcraft, they are never themselves accused because they have the strong support of their fellow Muslims and the local community. Nowadays Christians are increasingly the targets of such accusations. They are few in number and they tend to come from the lower social strata. They are also innovators who can be viewed as breaking with

[22] David Tait, *loc. cit.*

tradition: those living in glass houses are not best placed for throwing stones. Yet, as the survey shows, they are respected members of society, because they are seen as loving and helping everyone, even their enemies. The local or popular church has done all it can. People's identity as *Dagomba* can only be increased if the foreign-ness of the church is lessened. Like the Muslim leadership, the Catholics must come to the defense of church members in ways that respect the customs as they transform them.

Christ took the form of a slave so that we might be free. Nothing less than such radical service in love can transform the power of the chieftaincy (*naam*) and the de-humanising effects of victimization. Only the Gospel message can turn the contemporary power relations around; church and state politics have failed repeatedly. Development that merely aims at liberating women or insuring "minorities" their political and economic rights will only replace the old oppressors with new ones. *Dagomba* women are even now using their empowerment to secure their own security at the cost of community development,[23] while the "minorities" are furthering their own political ambitions by mirroring the old *naam*. Even now, politicians "settle" matters by instituting more chieftaincies. But the deeper freedom of the Gospel calls for the redemption of the *naam* itself. This will involve the transformation of an enslaving system into a system that frees through loving service. Thus the Gospel requires much more than simple justice: it asks for unreserved love. "Even the thieves can love those who love them." Christians must be resolute in loving those who persecute them. *Dagbon* may need a new Penitential Rite. Certainly radical conversion is called for.

The currently-advocated pastoral solution to witchcraft is too individual and too superficial: "Put yourself into the hands of God; pray with the person, and encourage him or her to trust God whose power is greater than that of witches or spiritual powers," said one priest at a local parish. Priests misunderstand the deeper issues when they only focus on the accused. Here too we see the results of the church's individualistic bias. The social dimensions must also be addressed. The problem arises not just from the spirit world but from deep within society. Despite their many weaknesses, the Christian Communities are responding to the deeper issues by their expressions of love. This is the authentic Christian antidote to witchcraft. But social evils also require communal action like protecting the accused, and rituals like communal fasting and prayer emphasizing joyful service. Even though Christians are at risk of being accused themselves, they courageously fulfill their role. It is only when

---

[23] Jon Kirby, "Why the *Anufo* Do Not Eat Frogmeat: The Importance of Taboo-making for Development," *Occasional Papers* (Tamale Institute of Cross-Cultural Studies, 1987), 1-13.

116

Christian communities come to the support of those accused, and love them along with their accusers, that Christ's redeeming love can be made manifest.

To Illumine the Path toward the "New Naam"

We have seen examples and possibilities for doing inculturation and creating new and more appropriate rituals; they are small beginnings and the process is not easy. Only by intense observation, involvement, and social and cultural analysis can the official church identify the central cultural themes of a people, which are the primary targets for social evangelization. In the case of *Dagbon*, a central theme is the chieftaincy (*naam*). If the Gospel is to be preached effectively, it must enter the heart of the *naam* where results have been so meager, for it is here more than anywhere that the *Dagomba* people long to experience the transforming power of Christ.

Inculturation depends on the cooperation of the popular church and the local official church. Thus far in Africa, the popular church has outstripped the advance of the official church. The first step in moving ahead is for church personnel to really discover what is happening at the grass roots, to look beyond stereotypes and to comprehend – through linguistic and cultural lenses – the social and religious dynamics of people's lives. Then perhaps, the official church can take appropriate steps to converge with the popular church. The onus for doing inculturation is thus now on the institutional local churches.

Inculturation is not an option. No less than the integrity of the church itself demands it. The Spirit is calling, and the church must follow the Spirit. A church and its ministry that fails to take inculturation seriously, and to promote an authentically contextualized Christianity in each local church, is not authentic. An inculturated church and ministry, with an appropriate Christian response to the politics of subjugation, are imperative if the demands of justice, democracy and human development in Africa are to be met. There is great urgency. Even the "minority" groups among whom the church seems to be enjoying current success, do not deny the chieftaincy (*naam*). They simply renounce their place at the bottom of the system. Not to sponsor inculturated ministry is to condone and perpetuate injustice. For without the model of Christian love illuminating a new path, many people will be every bit as ready to espouse the injustice of human exploitation as some of those currently in power and currently abusing authority, whether ecclesiastical, political or domestic.

QUESTIONS

1. Intense observation and social analysis provide a basis for authentic local churches. Equally important is a deep knowledge of theology and tradition. How might you, as a pastor, support this agenda? Consider practical approaches, and indicate a time-scale.

2. What is the difference between "Popular Catholicism" and dangerous syncretism?

3. The author urges cooperation between the official church and popular religion. But the *magisterium* sometimes appears very authoritarian, and "popular religion" is judged inferior, superstitious, and unorthodox. Suggest how authentic inculturation might be encouraged.

4. The underlying problems of witchcraft are not simply due to erroneous ideas about the spirit world, but are located deep within the society. This suggests a sociological explanation for witchcraft. How can such an understanding help the church to address witchcraft?

5. What do you think of a new penitential service? What about a new Penitential Rite?

CHAPTER SEVEN

BABY RITUALS, RITUAL BATHS, AND BAPTISM –
A CASE FROM CONGO

Piet Korse, M.H.M.

The Congo is the setting, and a priest from Holland is the guide for this chapter. Long experience, keen insight, and careful analysis are brought to bear on some rituals found among the Mongo people. Knowledge of local culture and liturgical tradition allow the author to interpret each of these to the other and suggest ways of promoting a more inculturated sacramental liturgy and catechesis. The chapter has intrinsic value, but also great potential as a stimulus to others working in other local churches.

Part One: Baby Rituals and Ritual Baths

Baby Rituals

Certain rituals (*wiko* or *jiko*) are performed by parents to strengthen their baby's health by providing protection from evil forces like bad spirits or witches, and insurance against all kinds of sickness. *Wiko* is also performed in order to prevent the baby being suddenly shocked, whether by the arrival of a witch, by the cry of a bird, or by the shadow of a tree.

Among the *Mongo*, the ritual protection of a baby starts when the mother is about three months pregnant. She and her husband come together in a special way very early in the morning, and the husband takes a branch of the very resistant *ikulu y'aende* tree, and ties it around his wife's belly. In this way he also takes responsibility for the pregnancy, thus preventing, it is believed, any involuntary abortion. Later in the pregnancy, the husband goes to the forest and tries to kill a particular bird with a plaintive cry (*mpwa* or *bonkon-koji*), which may cause the baby to have a fit. The bird's head will be kept safely at home.

In its first two months of life a baby is impervious to shock, because it neither notices what happens around it nor understands what is being said. But then it starts to react and is capable of getting frightened – and even losing consciousness! The people say that it has fainted (*aolikwa*). In order to prevent such fainting fits the parents have to perform two *wiko* ceremonies in the first two months. The first, which uses the head of the bird (*mpwa*), takes place two weeks after birth. It is performed very early in the morning, before dawn, when witches should have gone back home. People hope that the witches will also take with them any sickness or trace of witchcraft that might otherwise afflict the baby.

Before sunrise then, the parents come together, though not in a sexual way: they "unite their knees," symbolizing the union that produces a child, for the real protection of a baby's life started with the conjugal act, the "coming together of the knees." On this occasion, however, the parents must not complete their union lest the child become lazy, or even mad. The reason given is that if their father were to feel weak or tired after sex, and present himself in that state for the ceremony intended to strengthen the baby, he might pass on his own weakness.

Still before dawn, and before beginning any other task, the baby's mother leaves her bed and burns the head of the bird (*mpwa*). She puts the ashes in a banana leaf or in a leaf called *lolongote*. Then, she places the baby on her knees, either outside the house or in the kitchen. Her husband takes a razor blade and makes incisions on all the joints of the baby's body (wrists, ankles, knees, elbows), and at the base of the back. Next, he rubs the ashes into the incisions. The bird's head represents any bird which scares the baby. From now on the baby will no longer be surprised by the cries of birds and it will no longer fall ill as a consequence.

If the birth has already taken place but the husband has not obtained the head of a *mpwa*, he goes to the forest with a friend to look for a tree on which the bird in question is perched. He then collects some bark from the eastern and western sides of the tree. Returning to the village, he gives them to his wife who soaks them in a basin of water. That night husband and wife unite in the prescribed way. Early next morning they wash the baby with the water containing the bark. Then one of them throws the water towards the west, so that the setting sun may take along the ailments of the baby, and any associated witchcraft. They take bark from the eastern side of the tree, because that is where the sun rises each day, completely new: a baby washed in water with the bark from the eastern side of the tree will become as new, without any sickness, happy, and accompanied by good luck. On other occasions the father may go to the forest looking for a different tree (*boole*), again taking bark from the eastern and western sides.

This *wiko* ceremony may be called the classical or standard form. But there are numerous variations on this theme, indicating the central importance of *wiko* among the *Mongo*. Here we identify several other forms, noting common features. We will build upon these in the subsequent application. They were noted in the *Waka* and *Bokakta* regions, and it would be important to determine the provenance of other variants.

The Rite on the Road

A few days after his baby's birth, the father goes into the forest in search of a certain kind of bark. He or his wife takes a couple of banana leaves and scorches them lightly. The leaves are then placed in a basin into which water is poured. The baby's mother adds the bark to the water, together with some dead leaves of the *lolongote,* which they have previously used for their meals. She collects these leaves from the rubbish heap behind the kitchen.

The following night, when the whole village is asleep, parents and baby leave the house, carrying the basin with its contents, and move on to the road. In the rut made by the wheels of cars and bikes, the father digs a hole in which he spreads the banana leaves. On top of these leaves he pours the water containing the bark and the *lolongote* leaves. The mother then stands beside the hole, puts the baby on top of her feet and washes it, drawing water from the hole.

Interestingly, in this instance the night is understood to be propitious: objects from the forest and the kitchen area are immune from witchcraft, and even *fetishes* and objects that have been bewitched lose their power in this context. It is said that the child is washed on the road because then the dirt of the baby's body – including any trace of witchcraft – will be carried away by the vehicles' wheels and by the feet of passers-by.

Wiko behind the House

During the night the parents "unite their knees." Next morning the father goes in search of the *boole* tree (see above), a small anthill (*etuka*), and a palm tree sapling. These he keeps at home. The following night the process is repeated, and very early in the morning the parents take the baby and the objects the father has gathered the previous day. Behind the house the father digs a hole in which he spreads the banana leaves. On top of these he pours the water containing the bark. In this water he washes his private parts. Then the mother does the same, after which the father washes the baby thoroughly in the same water. To complete the ceremony, the parents together plant the small palm tree in the hole, placing the small black anthill next to it. Their hope is that, as the palm tree grows, so also will their baby grow, becoming strong and resistant like the anthill.

Washing the baby in the same water in which the parents washed, links it with the source of life and power which brought it to birth. And subsequently, after each sexual union the parents will touch the baby with the cloth with which they have dried their private parts.

Other Forms of *Wiko*

Enough has been said to provide a general view of *wiko*. There are many variations, of which we could mention the following:

Wiko on the roof of the house: When the standard *wiko* is ineffective, a medicine man may distill a liquid from a certain tree (*bolanga*), and at noon the parents administer it to their baby as eyedrops. The heat of the midday sun is a painful irritant to the baby, but also to any lingering malevolent spirits. The latter will be driven away, any sickness or contamination will remain on the roof, and the child will never be allowed to play up there.

Wiko on an anthill: The mother fills a gourd with water. No one must touch it. After "uniting the knees" with her, the father scrapes bark from the iron tree (*lolo*) in the prescribed way, and also gathers a small anthill and two banana leaves. Later, the parents with the child will climb on to a large termite hill. The digging of the hole, placing of leaves, pouring of water and personal washing are then followed by the father chewing the scrapings from the iron tree (*lolo*). Next, he pours water and expectorates the medicine on the baby's head as he blesses the child, saying: "Be blessed; and may no bewitching of this child ever be as powerful as the blessing of its parents." The mother then pours water on the baby's head in silence, and leaves the termite hill. The father puts the remaining medicine in the hole, which he seals with the small anthill. The rationale is this: the termite hill is large and cannot be moved. Any ailments or witchcraft associated with that place will remain there, and the child will be free. But the whole family must avoid it in future.

Wiko in the house or toilet: If the baby should lose consciousness it can be roused by pungent smells: the burnt hair and skin of a certain animal (*wunju*), or the noisome smell of an open-pit latrine, can work wonders!

Wiko beneath a banana tree: The father takes part of the banana flower, and the mother takes leaves, scorches them, and places them in a bowl. The father pours water into the bowl and crushes the banana flower into it. Having dug a hole at the foot of a banana tree, he returns home. The following dawn, after "uniting the knees," the parents return to the hole with their baby and the medicinal mixture. The baby is held vertically over the hole. The father pours water on the baby's head, and then the mother pours the mixture over the baby's body. Before leaving, the parents cover the hole with the water, symbolically containing any ailments afflicting the baby, with banana leaves and the bowl.

Wiko with nail clippings: The baby's hair and nails are clipped by an appropriate ritual figure, and these things are buried under any tree in the forest. "Uniting the knees" is a necessary prerequisite, as in other cases.

Wiko outside: The baby's father gathers the roots of a vine (*botofe*), a favorite of monkeys. Early in the morning, the mother sits with the baby on a stool (*ibolongo*), the root is burnt, and after the father has made two small incisions on the baby's chest and two more on the mother's thighs, the charcoal is rubbed into the incisions. Making four incisions on the baby's head, the father rubs charcoal into them. The charcoal may be kept for future use.

So much for *wiko*, with its components and variations. It is used to forestall or remedy attacks attributed to malevolent spirits; it requires both parents and the child; it takes place by stages, in the early evening, at night, at dawn; and it involves two critical components: symbolic sexual union and lustrations.

Ritual Baths

From rituals associated with babies, we now turn to those intended specifically for adults. We look at the baths intended to rid someone permanently from an ailment and from any bad spirit associated with it. Such rituals are performed at night in order to avoid the attention of witches. There are two sorts of baths (*totoke ts'otso*). One takes place on the river embankment so that the flow of the river will carry the sickness away. The other takes place on the road so that the feet of passers-by and the tires of vehicles and bicycles will carry the sickness away. This has already been described above. Here we simply add further observations.

If an illness lingers after normal remedies have been tried, the ritual bath may be prescribed. At midnight a healer takes the patient towards the river where he sacrifices a chicken, goat or dog. Before throwing the sacrifice into the river the healer makes the patient sit in the water. He then takes a dugout canoe, inverts it, and covers the patient with it. The patient will be unable to see how the crocodile receives and devours the sacrifice. While the dugout covers the patient, the sacrifice is thrown into the river and all contamination is carried away so that the patient can be healed. But the patient must leave without looking back.

Sometimes the sacrificial animal augurs the death of a family member: a few days later that person might fall ill and die.

If a woman is diagnosed as possessed (*jebola*), a female healer may take her at midnight to the road, where she will be made to sit on a piece of wood. The healer takes certain leaves, along with some pieces of bark from a tree (*bonkoonge*). They are put in a small basket (*eoko*), which is then placed on the patient's head. The healer takes water from a basin and pours it into the basket; the sap from the leaves and the bark flows over the whole body of the patient. Next, the healer takes the leaves and dries or rubs the patient's body with them. This takes away every trace of any bad spirits' presence. The patient then dresses and returns to the healer's home, where she sweeps the kitchen, gathers the ashes and throws them behind the house, saying: "Go for ever, don't come back again." The healer drops the leaves onto the road, but the piece of wood on which the patient was sitting is thrown far into the forest: the patient will never again encounter either the wood or the ailments. The bath water and the leaves are left on the road so that vehicles and passers-by will take away any sickness left on the road.

There are many other ritual baths, designed to chase away evil spirits and restore people to health. They require the ministrations of a healer, and appropriate leaves or other artifacts. Some of them, which are of particular relevance, are the following:

Ritual Purification Bath of a Widow

At dawn the officiant, assisted by two or three others, takes the widow to a brook or river. They carry a bar of soap, a razor blade, and new clothes. In the brook the officiant makes two dams, one downstream and the other upstream; the widow will be washed in the water between the dams. First the officiant cuts the widow's nails and shaves her head and entire body. She then invites the widow to move into the water, where she washes her with leaves from a particular tree (*bosifo*) and the soap brought for the occasion.

The officiant breaks the two dams so that the water flows downstream, carrying with it both the widow's clothes and all impurity. The widow will leave the stream without looking behind, while both she and the officiant shout: "Widowhood, go away along with the water."

The Ritual Bath of Twins (*bososo*)

This ceremony is performed when a twin falls ill and the ailment is attributed to the spirits who accompany twins. Symptoms include ulcers, swollen eyes and bleeding teeth. Twins are always accompanied by certain spirits, so this ceremony (*bososo*) is obligatory: the spirits have to be mollified by this ritual bath. The ceremony is performed for the first time at home when the mother comes out of seclusion, between four and seven days after birth.

Even before the *bososo*, there is another ceremony: on the very day of the twins' birth, the parents call upon another mother of living twins (*nalongo*). She pours water into a basin, adding white chalk (the color of spirits) to rejoice the twins' spirits. Taking two eggs, she makes a hole in them and lets a small amount of yoke drop into the water. Then taking two branches of a plant (*bonsonsole*), she dips these in the water and sprinkles the twins and their parents, touching them with the branches. She ties a few palm fronds around the necks of the twins and their parents. These signify that a person is a twin or a parent of twins. Then the lady cooks the two eggs and gives some to the twins. The rest is eaten by the parents and herself. Thus the twins and their spirits are calmed and made happy.

Returning now to the ritual bath (*bososo*): the day before the ceremony, the mother of twins who assisted on the day the new twins were born, asks their parents to provide two chickens (preferably white), or at least two eggs, two bottles of palm oil, some bananas, and two bank notes. On the following night the parents must avoid sexual relations – as is the case with the *wiko* ceremony – for three stated reasons. First, unlike other children, twins belong to spirits and are therefore very sensitive to outside influences. Second, sexual intercourse would cause the twins to fall ill. And third, the mother must be given time to recuperate from the twins' birth.

On the following day the mother of the other twins returns. The new parents give her what she had requested. She takes a chicken and hands it back to the parents: its eggs will be used if the twins become sick. She also hands back one bottle of palm oil, in which to fry the eggs for the twins. Then she carefully cuts each of the bananas in half, giving one part to the parents. Then the parents give one bank note to each twin. They may add small gifts such as two cups and saucers (one set for each twin), to humor their spirits.

Each parent then picks up a twin. They leave the house for the ritual bath, which takes place behind the house. The officiant digs two holes near the wall of the home, where rainwater falls from the roof. If, by bad luck, one of the twins has already died, she digs only one hole. Then, taking two banana leaves, she spreads them in the holes and pours water over them. She takes the remaining chicken, cuts its beak, and lets a few drops of blood fall into the holes. With the chicken in her hand she sprinkles all the walls of the home to rejoice the spirits of the twins. She puts some of the blood in the water, and will later sprinkle the twins: to sprinkle with chicken blood is to welcome and bless a person by imploring the protection of the ancestors. The twins will now be healthy and will jump up and down like the chicken.

Taking four branches of the plant *bonsonsole*, the officiant puts two in each hole. Because of its bad smell, this plant has the reputation of being able to chase away the bad spirits, and is a favorite in rituals. The officiant takes four branches from a tree (*liyamba*) and puts two in each hole. These will unite the parents with their twins (The word *liyamba* is related to *bamana,* meaning "to join"). She then traces a horizontal line on the foreheads of the twins and their parents with the chalk, as she drops the rest of it into the holes; the chalk is for protection and a sign of welcome to the spirits that accompany the twins.

Now, taking all the branches, she dips them into the water of both holes and sprinkles and touches first the mother and the twin she holds. All present sing and dance, while the mother turns round so that her whole body is sprinkled. The father, who holds the other twin, is sprinkled also. Then those assembled sing a song of joy and blessing for the twins and their parents.

Finally, the officiant tears up the banana leaves that she had spread in the holes. The holes, however, are not filled in as in other rites, because the spirits might believe the twins have been buried. Open holes indicate life; the spirits are happy and will provide the twins with good health. Everyone now returns to the house. The officiant brings along the palm branches and destroys them. The small palm fronds are tied around the necks of the twins and their parents. The twins' mother prepares the chicken that was killed during the ceremony, using the palm oil and bananas. The cooked chicken liver is put to the lips of the twins, so that they participate; the parents and the officiant eat the rest.

Part Two: Application

With the foregoing information in mind, we now consider Christian baptism among the *Mongo,* offering suggestions about the liturgical form and administration of the sacrament intended to help it resonate with *Mongo* experience. Beyond this, we offer a catechesis intended to help communities where Christian baptism is relatively new. We will identify and emphasize two themes: at the individual level, exorcism and the beginning of a new life; and at the community level the creation and perpetuation of the People of God, the church.[1]

---

[1] Each specific suggestion – whether for a modification of or an addition to current liturgical practice, will be marked individually (by an arrow). This might help readers who are themselves trying to deal with the inculturation of the liturgy.

As we noted, many *Mongo* rites are designed to remove everything that contaminates a person, whether spirit possession, witchcraft, or more general forms of pollution. Water is an element found in many rites. But water is not to be used casually. Water for ritual use is not just ordinary water. It should not remain in the village after use. It has to disappear, to signify the definitive disappearance of the particular evil it opposes. There are several ways of disposing of the lustral water, including the following: allowing it to be swept away by the current; "burying" it in a hole; letting it be carried away by passing traffic (pedestrian or vehicular); using it to water a banana tree or a palm tree; throwing it towards the setting sun; "locking" it in a hole covered by a small black anthill to prevent evil returning and to signify the power of new life; or throwing it onto the roof to signify the rapid disappearance of the sickness.

➤ Consistent with all this, we suggest that the baptismal water should likewise be disposed of after the sacrament has been administered. This would palpably signify the departure of evil and the power of new life.

In the early church people were baptized in a river or a brook (Ac 8:36-39; Rm 6:3; Col 2:12; Eph 5:26; Tit 3:5). However, as the church expanded, inculturation took place as cultures in colder or drier climates were evangelized. Certainly in Europe, and especially in winter, it makes little sense to immerse people in icy waters. Other regions may not have had rivers or brooks. And so it was that immersion became transformed into a simple pouring of water on the catechumen's head. One might say that baptism became more and more symbolic, or that one symbol was replaced by another even though the second was not as clear a signifier as the first. It is surprising that until quite recently the church retained this vestige of inculturation – the pouring of water at baptism – as one of the few rituals prescribed for the universal church.

Here are some lines from the *Didache*, written at the end of the first century: "Baptize in the name of the Father and of the Son and of the Holy Spirit, in running water. If you have no running water, baptize in other water. If you cannot stand cold water, do it in warm water. If you do not have either, pour water three times on the head in the name of the Father and of the Son and of the Holy Spirit" (7). The *Letter of Barnabas*, written around the year 120 CE, simply speaks of "going down into the water" (11:8-11).

➤ We may ask whether this European form of baptism is appropriate for equatorial regions. Wherever a great number of baths take place in streams, should the church not revert to the earlier practice and baptize again in streams? Then the desire to see the spirit of evil driven from one's life once and for all would be expressed and understood more clearly. Yet even baptism by immersion is only one of several possibilities for baptism. What if it were conferred behind the church, or inside the church but using some vernacular meanings? We could consider the following:

Baptism behind the Church

➢ After the first part of the ceremony has taken place in the church, the baptismal party processes round to the back of the building where the minister, parent, or godparent digs a hole. A banana leaf will be placed in it, and on this leaf will be poured the water used in the actual baptism. According to custom, a banana leaf is appropriate because the banana tree grows quickly. First, a prayer is offered, asking for rapid and healthy growth for the newly baptized. Then the (god)parent places the banana leaf in the hole and the priest calls down God's power on the catechumen, asking that the child may grow in faith and come to accept responsibilities in the community.

➢ The head of the catechumen is now bowed over the hole as the baptismal water is poured over the head and allowed to flow into the hole. Later, the godfather will symbolically "bury" the water, marking the definitive departure of sin. At the end of the rite, a banana tree will be planted in the hole. Among the *Mongo* there are already rites that could be adapted by the Christian community to ask God's blessing and the rapid growth of the baptised.

➢ The banana tree has a double significance, pointing both to death and to life: such trees frequently grow on garbage dumps or where decaying vegetable matter has been thrown. The planting of a banana tree in the hole where the baptismal water flowed would signify the end of a life under the power of sin and the beginning of a new life in the power of the Spirit. The family of the newborn child can be enjoined to watch and care for the banana tree, just as they watch and care for the baptized child who has new life in the Spirit. In the *wiko* ceremonies, a palm tree rather than a banana tree is planted. But after birth, and in the case of a possessed woman (*jebola*), people prefer a banana tree. It is a more powerful symbol of rapid growth and points to a sensational improvement of the patient's health.

➢ If a banana tree has been planted on the spot where the baptismal water flowed, a further celebration might likewise take place when it bears fruit. This already happens in the ceremonies for a possessed woman (*jebola*), and something similar takes place a year after the birth of a baby. On both those occasions a healer is called, and on the occasion of a baby's birthday, the grandmother also. Everyone eats the bananas in a joyful atmosphere.

So when the banana tree planted on the day of baptism comes to fruition, a special meal could be arranged. The priest and godparents might be invited to this "catechetical moment," at which the community of the baptized could be underscored once again.

➤ To conclude the baptism itself, the priest could take a small black anthill – its hardness symbolizing resistance – and put it at the foot of the newly-planted banana tree, as a reminder to everyone that the forces of evil must never be taken lightly, and that following Christ is a lifetime's work.

Baptism inside the Church

Even if baptism is conferred inside the church, some rites used outside the building could be included. Baptism (especially for adults) might look something like the following:

➤ During the ceremony the catechumen faces the East, symbolic of the desire for the fullness of the gifts of new life: Christ is the new sun whose rising brings all that is good. At the conclusion of the ceremony, the baptismal water, collected in a basin, is thrown onto the road in order that all evil be carried away. Or it is poured into a hole in which a banana tree is planted, or thrown in the direction of the setting sun which carries away all evil.

➤ In lustral rites the purified person must not look back: similarly, at the end of the baptismal rite the officiant can ask the baptized to leave the place of baptism without looking back – a sign of determination to leave behind all that is evil and to make a definite decision for Christ.

➤ As a mark of new life, in some rituals those who have been washed leave their old clothes behind and dress in new ones. Immediately after baptism the neophyte could put on new clothes and then come back for the rest of the ceremonies.

➤ In the traditional baptismal ceremony the baptized is anointed on those parts of the body judged particularly significant: the back, the chest and the forehead. *Wiko* ceremonies indicate that the *Mongo* identify the vital parts of the body rather differently. For them the joints are particularly significant: wrists, ankles, neck, elbows, shoulders and knees. To these one has to add the forehead, the space between the eyes, the temples near the top of the ear, and the base of the spine. To anoint these places with holy oils would be to sanctify and to protect the whole human being against evil influences.

➤ The holy oils could be administered in the following way: before the actual baptism, the father of the baptized would make some incisions (the number depending on the region) on the wrists, knees, elbows, neck, shoulders, and the base of the back. The priest would rub the holy oil into the incisions whilst praying the Holy Spirit to come and protect and strengthen the newly baptized. After the baptism, the father would make some incisions on the forehead of the baptized. The priest would then take the chrism and rub it into the incisions whilst praying that the thoughts of the baptized be directed toward the love and life shown by Christ Jesus. Then the father would make some incisions on the temples, and the priest would rub in the holy oil while praying that the ears of the baptized be open to the message of Christ, to the signs of the times, and to the teachings of the church.

➢ Instead of the traditional exorcism during which the priest blows in the direction of the catechumen and orders the devil to leave, one could employ the local method of applying eye drops. The *Mongo* make eye drops from the young leaves of the *bolanga* tree and apply them to a sick baby so as to chase away any evil. Eye drops may also protect against evil influences generally. At the beginning of the baptismal ceremony, therefore, after the parents and godparents have been asked why they are there, the baby's father could apply the eye drops while the priest asks the devil to leave this place to the Holy Spirit.

➢ During the treatment of a possessed woman (*jebola*), the sick person is placed on a scaffold. Underneath, a fire is lit so that the smoke envelops the patient. Then the spirits of the ancestors start to speak through the patient, indicating which rules are to be observed so that the healing process can be completed. Likewise, in the life of the newly baptized, the forces of evil will not leave unless the great commandment is observed: to love God and neighbor. To express this idea, the priest would take a thurible and have the catechumen bow before the font. The priest would hold the smoking thurible under the catechumen's face whilst saying: "If you want to obtain eternal life, observe the commandments: love the Lord, your God, with your whole heart, your whole soul, your whole spirit and your whole strength. And love your neighbor as yourself. For there is no greater commandment than these two." The catechumens and the choir would then sing an appropriate hymn.

Becoming Part of God's People

Baptism is not only a ritual bath but the door through which one enters into the sanctuary of God's people. In the current liturgy of baptism this entrance into the Christian community is poorly expressed. But bearing in mind the importance the Congolese church attaches to Small Christian Communities, it is necessary to underline this aspect of baptism. By baptism a person becomes part of God's people and incurs certain responsibilities; but the community in turn has a responsibility towards the baptized.

As representatives of the Christian community, we may identify two categories or groups of people: the parents (in the case of infant baptism), who are primarily responsible for faith formation; and the godparents, catechist, parish representatives, and the minister of baptism.

First consider the parents. Quite commonly these days the child's father is more or less an outsider at the baptism. Sometimes he is not even present but leaves the job to his wife. But given the important place he takes in the *wiko* ceremonies – where the active presence of both parents is indispensable – his presence at baptism is certainly called for. At baptism the active participation of parents could be expressed in several ways.

➢ The night before baptism they could come together in the way prescribed by the *wiko* ceremonies. Thus it will become clear to them that they are responsible for the child's education and of his/her growth in the faith.

➢ As the *Didache* puts it: "Before baptism, both the one who baptizes as well as the candidate for baptism fast, together with those who can do so." Could we not ask the (adult) candidate to fast one or two days before baptism, and perhaps the parents or godparents?

➢ Before baptism the father could be asked to gather banana leaves, a banana tree, a black anthill, a razor blade, some white cloth, white chalk, and so on. Then again, the father could make the incisions on the child so that the child benefits most from the holy oils.

➢ Both parents could pronounce a blessing over the child by spraying water on its head and rubbing in the saliva. They could do this after the conferring of baptism. Also after the baptism, the father might perhaps tie a string with a medal around the middle of the child whilst the mother holds the baby.

➢ In the *wiko* ceremonies the father goes into the forest and collects some bark from the tree upon which he has seen a *mpwa* bird perched. In the same way the father could, the day before baptism, collect bark from a tree upon which a dove or wood pigeon was perched: the dove symbolizing the Holy Spirit. The father would then put the bark in water that will be used for baptism, thus expressing his desire for the coming of the Spirit in power (bark from the east side) and for the chasing away of all that is bad including the bad habits, innate or acquired (bark from the west side).

➢ In the rituals for twins, white chalk is used to appease the spirits and to protect the twins against all sorts of sicknesses; and while the twins are still children, traces of white chalk are put on their foreheads every day. During the baptismal rite, the priest could bless the white chalk for it to be a sign of the Holy Spirit, and trace a cross on the foreheads of the baptized while asking the Holy Spirit to always accompany the children of

God and to protect them against all evil. The parents could continue this practice from time to time.

➤ At the beginning of the baptismal rite the minister could address the parents by asking concrete questions concerning the education of their child: are they ready to teach the common prayers, to bring the child to Sunday service and catechism class, to teach the love of God and neighbor, and to give the child its place in the Basic Christian Community and in the parish?

We should not forget the godparents, the catechist, and the leader of the local community. They are the representatives of the local Christian community. They receive new members into the community.

➤ They should have the right to ask – especially in the case of adult baptisms – certain questions to see whether the candidate fulfills the required conditions. Questions might include: are you ready to be part of the Christian community? Are you willing to participate in the construction of God's Kingdom among us? Are you ready to participate in our prayers, to help the poor, to be part of any activity proposed by our local community, to follow the instructions for first communion and to take on some responsibilities in the community? Thus one could omit the old questions concerning the renunciation of Satan and his works – questions which seem rather negative and abstract. Then in the name of those who want baptism, one of the three representatives of the local community could ask the priest to baptize them, calling their names and the names of the parents and the villages of origin. The godparents would also be presented: thus the importance of each person in the community would be underlined.

➤ Finally, the priest would ask the representatives of the community if they are ready to support the new members on their faith journey: to inspire them to follow Christ, to encourage them in their difficulties, to be ready to give them responsibilities in the communities in accordance with the charism of each of them.

➤ The objects necessary for the liturgy would then be brought in procession while people sing and dance. One procession might include those to be baptized, the godparents, the community's representatives and the priest. Different persons would hold the eye drops, holy oils, razor blade, the list with the names of the catechumens and so on. A second procession, just before the actual baptism, made up of the same people, would bring a spade or hoe, banana leaves, baptismal water, black anthills, white chalk, white cloths, and banana saplings. A third procession, immediately after baptism, is the solemn entry of the newly baptized in their new clothes. Each procession would come in singing and dancing.

QUESTIONS

1. The author provides a mass of detail about *Mongo* culture. Do you find it enlightening and helpful? What can it contribute to the inculturation of the liturgy? How might it be used to prevent some cultural misunderstandings among *Mongo* people exposed to the current Roman Rite for baptism?

2. What can theologians and ministers learn from this chapter about the importance of ethnographic inquiry and explanation? What is the significance of expressions of sexuality in terms of inculturation?

3. The author provides vernacular translations for objects and behavior. Why is this important? How could it be helpful for people *not* working among the *Mongo?*

4. Using this chapter as a model, can you identify cultural practices among other African groups, in such a way as to undertake the kind of sacramentalization of life and inculturation of the liturgy that Piet Korse attempts?

5. Inculturation requires knowledge of both ethnography and theology, or culture and liturgy. What is your assessment of the practical suggestions (marked with arrows in the text) for liturgical inculturation?

CHAPTER EIGHT

INCULTURATION AND PROVERBS FROM DAGBANI, GHANA

Kofi Ron Lange, S.V.D.

With more than three decades' experience in Ghana, the author of this chapter is particularly qualified to offer instruction. Traditional wisdom may not be written in books, but it does need to be retained; proverbs are one of the ways people express and transmit their deepest values. Jesus employed familiar proverbs in his teaching. As Christianity encounters different cultures, it should be able to identify and use their treasure-store of proverbial wisdom.

Introduction

Inculturation is a key term in theology and missiology. It – or a derivative – was probably first used in a theological sense by Joseph Masson SJ, in 1962. He said: "Today there is a more urgent need for a Catholicism that is *inculturated* in a variety of forms."[1] Though the word might be relatively new, the process to which it refers has a much longer history: it is as old as the faith, because the faith is always – at least to some degree – expressed in the cultural and linguistic forms of the people who profess it. For example, in Hebrew culture the word which was originally used for a Bedouin's tent and later for a stone or brick home is translated "temple" in a religious setting; and the word for a king's palace becomes the name for the holy place of the temple area.

Aylward Shorter himself offers this definition: "Inculturation is the on-going dialogue between faith and culture or cultures."[2] This process refers not only to the first insertion of the Gospel into a hitherto non-Christian culture, but also to cultures in Europe and elsewhere, where the faith has been previously proclaimed and rooted. Since culture should be seen as a developing process rather than a static reality, this entails a continuous dialogue between faith and culture among people and between groups of all nations.

Inculturation must be based on partnership and mutuality. The Gospel [what is proclaimed] and the faith [what is professed] has the potential to transform a culture; but it is also true that Christianity is itself transformed

---

[1] Quoted in Aylward Shorter, *Toward a Theology of Inculturation* (London: Geoffrey Chapman, 1988), 10.

[2] Shorter, *op. cit.*, 11.

by culture. That is, the ways in which the message is formulated, interpreted and lived anew, are all derivatives of acculturation, the process whereby the encounter of two cultures inevitably affects each of them to a degree. Christianity should actually be enriched by the values of the culture that is being evangelized.

In other words, every new inculturation is a process whereby a new way of being Christian, a new way of being church, is brought into existence. The idea was stated quite explicitly by Pope Paul VI in one of the most often-quoted parts of *Evangelii Nuntiandi*:

> ... a church *toto orbe diffusa* would become an abstraction if it did not take body and life precisely through the individual churches. Evangelization loses much of its force if it does not take into consideration the actual people to whom it is addressed, if it does not use their language, their signs and symbols, if it does not answer the questions they ask, and if it does not have an impact on their concrete life. Legitimate attention to individual churches cannot fail to enrich the Church (*EN* 62, 63).

Wisdom and Wisdom Figures

The Christian faith can only be lived and expressed through human culture and human language. In Northern Ghana the *Dagomba* live in their traditional state, *Dagbon*. They are a sub-group of the *Gur* speaking peoples of northern Ghana and Togo and southern Burkina Faso. They are quite closely related – historically-culturally-linguistically – to four *Mole-Dagbani* peoples: the *Mamprusi, Nanumba, Mossi* and *Wala*.

The *Dagomba* world, like that of other societies in Ghana and Africa, is inhabited by humans, ancestors, spirits and deities. But *Dagomba* people also believe in the Supreme Being (*Naawuni*), Creator of all things. Their view of deity is pyramidal: the Supreme Being manifests the power of divinity through a hierarchy of spiritual entities beginning with lesser deities (*wuna*). Below these in the hierarchy are ancestral spirits (*yanima*) who have close ties with the living, blessing those who observe their teachings and ways, and punishing those who fail to show respect. At the base of the superhuman order are charms and amulets (*gurima*), imbued with power by deities or spirits, and used for defensive or offensive purposes.

People make themselves known through language. For special occasions or special purposes *Dagomba* people use special language: oral art is a special language. People who still live in the traditional way, as many *Dagomba* do, are masters of oral art, in which words and sounds, stories, riddles and songs – but especially proverbs – are used not only to communicate messages of immediate importance but also to reveal, establish and develop relationships between people at a deeper level. In fact, if we want a new definition of a proverb we could say, with Xavier Plissart: "A proverb is mainly a revealer of relationships and the consequences of relationships." Such relationships include those through which elders pass cultural wisdom to the younger generation; encourage positive values and discourage their opposites; and show and gain respect, reputation and status in the community as statesmen and "cultured" persons. In Western societies one sign of a cultured person is that such a one is educated and well read. In African society by contrast, a "cultured" person is the one who knows the cultural history of the people and is able to express him or herself with wit and humor through the use of proverbs, stories, metaphors, songs, and so on.

Proverbs in Africa are highly valued and used on a daily basis, in discussions between chiefs and elders, in the settling of disputes, and in the upbringing of children. In *Dagbon,* proverb authorship is ascribed to the elders in general. Some authors are actually known, but even so, when a proverb is used it is often introduced with the following words: "the elders say (give) the proverb." Proverb usage is the domain *par excellence* of the community elders; their age and social position qualifies them to pass down traditional matters and wisdom.

In the following section I will present some *Dagomba* proverbs as utterances that illuminate, illustrate, or reveal the message contained in the Bible and that can be used in Christian preaching and teaching.

The Significance of Proverbs

The message of proverbs is relevant to particular times and situations. In Ghana a person who wants to learn proverbs will go and ask an older person for instruction. The elder will say: "Close your eyes"; then after a few moments the elder says: "Now open your eyes and tell me what you saw." The usual answer is "nothing," to which the elder responds: "If you haven't slept, you cannot dream." The message of proverbs is eminently adaptable to different circumstances or situations. Proverbs are not immutably fixed in meaning: the non-permanency of each use of a proverb leaves room for continuous readjustment and change.

People use proverbial language as a kind of indirect reference or a way of relating to each other without being too precise, in order to avoid offending. They also want to avoid "rubbing against someone." As one proverb puts it: "The branch that is next to its neighbor is the one that rubs against it."

In *Dagomba* society, proverbs are seen and used as a means of saving face. To give too direct a message, either to or about a person who has transgressed the accepted cultural way of thinking or acting, is to cause that person to lose face or to be disgraced. This would be taken to mean you don't respect that person. Respect is the glue that holds *Dagomba* society together. The exchanging of respect makes the hierarchy of power and status visible and desirable. Respect is shown in the appropriate greetings and their responses at home, in the chief's palace, at the market, to the elders, at funerals, and at a variety of celebrations. When appropriate or expected respect is not forthcoming in all these situations – and in many others too – the person who fails to show respect will be looked down upon and condemned. This will often be done by means of a proverb such as: "If the thigh grows bigger than the calf of the leg, it means it has become infected." Even as one refrains from stating this proverb in personal terms such as: "If *your* leg is bigger ...," one is helping in the face-saving process. The use of a proverb in many situations will get the point across even more forcefully because the person offending knows that if he doesn't take heed of the veiled reference, something really serious will happen to him later that could disgrace him in the community.

Knowledge of the meanings of innumerable proverbs becomes part of a storehouse of wisdom that is passed down from elders to their juniors. The proverbs are the wealth and wisdom of the elders, and are not learned either by rote or in isolation. Once learned, they are actually used rather than simply retained in the memory: they are often incorporated into a discourse. A person uses a proverb in order to reveal something. Proverbs moreover are living wisdom, not merely fossils: people adept in their use can modify existing proverbs.

People may even create proverbial sayings which might subsequently gain acceptance, because of their attractive form and their capacity to make a point or reveal a hidden truth. I myself coined a new proverb while working among the *Kwahus* in 1969: "If a white man is in need, he will even ride in a tro tro" (*Ehia oburoni a, otena tro tro mu*). A *tro tro* is a truck [*maame* lorry or "mammy wagon" in other parts of Africa] with several planks used as seats and one of the cheapest means of transportation. These trucks are also called "bone crackers" because they are so uncomfortable to ride in. This proverb reveals that the *Kwahus* view all white people as rich and think that whites would never ride in a *tro tro* unless they were in dire need. Because of the imagery, this proverb was accepted, appreciated and enjoyed.

138

The Genius of Proverbial Wisdom

Language is a defining characteristic of humanity. It has always exercised a fascination over human beings, and is full of mystery and power. To name something is to have power over it; to utter appropriate language is to change the world. The oracle, the spell, the curse, the blessing – utterances of many kinds – all play an important role in human society. A sense of the mystery and power of language can be seen when one observes children's games, engages in fairy tales and folklore, or uses language performatively.[3]

In the book of Genesis the naming of things is equivalent to their being called into existence. This is the performative use of language: God spoke and things came to be (Gn 1:3-27). Islam also has a tradition similar to this: if one were to stumble on the right word and speak it, the whole universe would vanish in a moment.[4] When the elder uses a proverb, ordinarily nothing is said against it. The final verdict has been given. When the appropriate person, elder or chief, has spoken, a spokesperson says: "The chief has spoken, the case is finished." Only if another elder has a cleverer proverb will anything be said in response to the first one.

The spoken word is extremely powerful. In earlier times in *Ashanti,* if a person was going to be executed, the executioner (*obrafo*) would put a small knife (*sepow*) through both cheeks of the condemned person, piercing the tongue; thus he could not utter a curse against anyone. In Genesis we find that God created man in God's own image, and this includes the capacity to speak: to name and to communicate. God explicitly gave Adam the task of naming the creatures and, in some fashion, actually calling them into life (Gn 2:19-20).

Particularly since the Enlightenment of the eighteenth century, Western Christianity has tended to favor the rational proposition, which has achieved some prominence and dominance in preaching and teaching. "The good sermon" came to be identified as one with three points in logical sequence, followed by a logical conclusion. St. Paul, however, used the style of Hellenistic diatribe – in which he stimulates objectors and inquirers, and answers their questions and objections – because it was a current genre of discourse and would communicate his message more effectively than other forms of communication.

---

[3] For *performativity*, see J. L. Austin, *How to Do Things with Words* (Cambridge: Harvard University Press, 1962).

[4] Amos Wilder, *Early Christian Rhetoric: The Language of the Gospel* (Cambridge: Harvard University Press, 1971), 6.

The roots of the Old Testament, we may recall, were in oral recital and chant. Transmission was dependent on memory. Orality and oral tradition also had a powerful influence on, and were used extensively by, the Fathers of the church. "Even when the Gospels had long been in existence the Fathers frequently cited the words and deeds of Christ, not from these writings but from the still growing oral tradition, often in a somewhat different version."[5] In fact, Origen held the view that the Gospel as the Word of God is properly addressed to the ear and is not written for the eye. The Pharisees had always been strong advocates of the oral Torah. They taught that the Torah, as constitutive of God's living word, must not be allowed to become fixed and fossilized in the written form. This understanding and attitude remains widespread in Africa. A contemporary instance can be seen among the *Achode* people in the northern part of the Volta Region in Ghana. It is related to the cult of the deity *Burukung*. No person who can read and write is eligible for membership in this cult. It is taboo to write down anything concerning *Burukung*.

However, it would be inappropriate to elaborate the oral/written distinction in the early church at the expense of another contrast: communication should be personal rather than impersonal, first-hand rather than second-hand, and direct rather than indirect. The reason for this was that the Gospel or good news was intended to be shared with people by way of encounter rather than simply as the communication of information. The oral mode was particularly suited to this form of communication; the life-changing news about Jesus Christ, his miracles, and especially his resurrection, was being shared with new believers.

Applications

What comparisons can be drawn between the written and oral discourse forms of the Gospels, and contemporary *Dagbani* discourse? Even today the main mode of discourse among *Dagomba* people is oral. Not only *what* is said is important but *how* it is said: how the particular oral forms are used. The *Dagomba* expect an elder to speak of everyday events with metaphors, stories, innuendoes, proverbs, and historical allusions to their culture. In the Gospels we find that Jesus told stories that were very human and realistic. The persons in question, the scenes, the actions are not always religious in a formal or conventional sense. But Jesus always gives a moral and religious application to his stories. They are shaped toward a direct personal appeal or challenge.

---

[5] Wilder, *op. cit.*, 40.

This is sometimes made explicit by introductions such as "listen!" or conclusions like "Whoever has ears to hear, let them hear!" In Africa, the use of stories, proverbs, and so on, is not simply to entertain the people but above all to move them to hear (*wum*), which means not just physically hearing but being prepared to bring one's speech and actions in line with what the elder has just spoken.

The composers of the New Testament used the idioms and images and situations and stories that naturally came to hand, as the materials with which to shape their accounts and set forth the faith. How could they do otherwise? The good news itself was about God-made-man: about incarnation, embodiment, the enfleshing of divinity, not to say the divinization of the flesh! The Word of God is an eternal word spoken in everyday language; Jesus speaks Aramaic, the speech of family and friends and hearth and heath. Vernacular languages are the primary means of verbal communication and the means by which the first enduring world is built up. The images and metaphors are never exotic or bizarre but elemental and appropriate: they are the windows to the soul of a people, or the gates to an understanding of other worlds. We must necessarily understand, value, and employ them in our speaking, teaching and proclaiming of the good news of Jesus Christ. With this in mind, ten *Dagbani* proverbs are set side by side with ten Biblical references. This correlation may help us to see a kind of *dynamic equivalence* that is possible and indeed desirable if the good news is to be inculturated among the *Dagomba* and others who are not Semitic peoples of previous millennia but African peoples of today.

Proverbs and Biblical Corollaries

The following proverbs are arranged in this order: line one is an English translation of the *Dagbani* original (line two). If necessary, a summary or clarification of the meaning may come in line three between square brackets. The indented lines give biblical references.

➤ "Nobody sits on an elephant and then his feet drag on the ground."
{Ninsal' ku ba wobigu ka o gbaya lan vu tina}
[If we depend on Jesus, he will protect us from harm]

"The Lord is on my side, I will not fear" (Ps 118:6).

➤ *"Dust on one's feet is better than dust on one's buttocks."*
  {Napon tam so la gbinn' tam}

> "We hear that some among you are idle. They are not busy; they are busybodies. Such people we command and urge in the Lord Jesus to settle down and earn the bread they eat" (2 Thess 3:11).

➤ *"What an old man sits down and sees, a child climbs a tree to see – and still can't see."*
  {Ninkurugu ni zi tina ka nya sheli bii yi du tia o ku tooi nya li}

> "Honor your father and your mother that you may live long in the land the Lord your God is giving you" (Ex 20:12; Mt 15:4; 19:19 and parallels).

> "Jesus knew that the time had come for him to leave this world and go to the Father" (Jn 13:1).

> "You do not understand what I am doing but later you will understand" (Jn 13:7).

➤ *"The shade of a palm tree is not directly under it."*
  {Ninsal' kpukpalaga o mahim bi lur' o gbinni}
  [The meaning of things is not always immediately evident or easily understood]

> "None of the disciples dared ask him, 'who are you?' They knew it was the Lord" (Jn 21:12).

> "When he was at table with them, he took bread, said thanks, broke it and began to give it to them. Then their eyes were opened and they recognized him at first sight" (Lk 24:30).

➤ *"Even a group of a hundred elephants can not push a mountain."*
  {Wobri layim kobiga ku daai zoli}

> "For nothing is impossible with God" (Lk 1:37).

➤ *"Last year's koringa birds are showing this year's koringa birds how to disturb farmers when they are sowing seeds."*
  {Yuuni koringa n-wuhiri yuuni no koringa chi kpaybu}

> "But if anyone causes one of these little ones who believe in me to sin, it would be better for that one to have a large millstone hung around his neck and to be drowned in the depths of the sea" (Mt 18:6).

➤ *"If you are giving water to a lazy man's goat, the goat is still the lazy man's goat."*
{A yi nyuhiri vinnyayulan' bu' kom, o bu' nye la o bua}

"You who preach against stealing, do you steal?" (Eph 2:21).

"You shall not steal" (Ex 20:15).

➤ *"If you have patience you can put a cloth in a narrow-neck gourd."*
{Suyulo yi bieni chinchini ni kpe gayili ni}

"We do not want you to become lazy, but to imitate those who through faith and patience inherit what has been promised" (Heb 6:12).

"You have heard of Job's patience and have seen what the Lord has finally brought about" (Job 1:21-22).

➤ *"If a person is whistling a tune, later on he will sing the song."*
{Nir' yi vulim' vulinga o ni lan yili di yila}

"What the heart is full of, the mouth speaks" (Mt 12:34).

"For out of the heart comes evil thoughts, murder, adultery, sexual immorality, theft, false testimony, slander" (Mt 15:19).

➤ *"An unbroken egg doesn't know what is inside it."*
{Nongalli muni ku ban naa ni}
[People don't realize that they are made in the image and likeness of God]

"God said, 'Now we will make humans and they will be like us'" (Gen 1:26).

[Do Christians realize their dignity as sons and daughters of God?]

"You are a chosen priesthood, a holy nation, a people belonging to God, that you may declare the praises of the one who called you out of darkness into his wonderful light" (1 Pet 2:9).

QUESTIONS

1. Does this chapter help persuade you of the importance of aspects of oral wisdom as a component of inculturation? How will you become familiar with the study of orality?

2. Identify some of the proverbs used by Jesus, then discuss the use of local proverbs as a means of catechesis.

3. If proverbs are largely held and circulated by the elders, can a missionary expect to become conversant with, and a user of such oral forms? Under what circumstances might one produce acceptable new proverbs, as the author did?

4. Identify some proverbs from your own cultural tradition. Show how they may be used as a means of evangelization.

5. Assuming the material in this chapter is already familiar to you, what modifications can you suggest?

CHAPTER NINE

"TEARS A-PLENTY" –
SONGS OF SUFFERING IN CENTRAL AFRICA

Xavier Plissart, M. Afr.

*Inculturation can only happen in concrete and particular circum-
stances. The following account exemplifies a kind of spontaneous
inculturation, something that could never have been planned. Yet it
is traceable to the pre-existing action of nature and of grace. It illustrates the possibilities open to communities of faith. If local situations
produce local problems, cannot local churches discover authentic local
solutions?*

The Context

In this chapter I will illustrate the fact that any commitment to inculturation requires an awareness of and respect for the constraints of contextualization. Inculturation is a *process* rather than an event, and it develops in
particular times and places. Failure to understand temporal and spatial dynamics will inhibit and perhaps seriously undermine the integrity of the
process. We will look at the place and the time, and the words and the deeds,
of Mgr. Christophe Munzihirwa who died in October 1996 in Bukavu (former
Zaïre), a martyr for the truth. As we come to understand how his testimony
was received by a group of young people who formed the "Lavigerie Choir," we
might perhaps better understand some of the dynamics of inculturation. A
short and simplified historical survey will provide important background material.

The Legacy

Before the colonial era, the region now formed by Rwanda and Burundi,
two small countries in central Africa, was ruled by a minority ethnic group of
non-Bantu origin: the *Batutsi* pastoralists. The colonial administration cooper-
ated with the *status quo*, but with the advent of democracy after independence
in the 1960s, the Bantu majority – the *Bahutu* – came to power in both
countries. As a consequence, many *Tutsi* were discriminated against and either
chose – or were forced – to take refuge abroad. A large group settled in southern
Uganda and many of their young men joined the army of Museveni in the
guerilla war against Idi Amin Dada. Their presence was particularly strong in

the army's secret service. When Museveni seized power, these young men formed the backbone of an armed group whose main aim would be the restoration of *Tutsi* rule in "their" territories. Gradually, since 1990, under the leadership of U.S. trained Paul Kagame, they invaded Rwanda from the north. They later presented themselves also as a political party called the *Front Patriotique Rwandais* (*FPR*), and as such entered negotiations in Arusha (Tanzania) for political power-sharing, while continuing the reconquest.

In April 1994, the *Hutu* presidents of Rwanda and Burundi were killed when the plane in which they traveled was shot down coming in to land in Kigali. *Hutu* extremists in Rwanda were frustrated by the inability of their leaders and the army (*Forces Armées Rwandaises,* or *FAR*) to resist the invasion. They had set up their own militia, the *interahamwe.* When their president was killed they unleashed of spate of systematic massacres of *Tutsi* collaborators and *Hutu* moderates in Rwanda. This genocide accounted for around 500,000 people.[1]

Nevertheless, the *FPR* continued its advance, and in July 1994 took power in Kigali. During the genocide, thousands of *Tutsi* and moderate *Hutu* fled across the borders, especially to the towns of Goma and Bukavu in eastern Zaïre. These were then followed by an enormous crowd composed of members of the *Hutu* armed forces (*FAR*), members of the defeated *Hutu* militia (*interahamwe*), and hundreds of thousands of implicated or innocent civilians who feared, with good reason, the merciless retaliation of the soldiers of the *FPR*.

Meanwhile, in 1995, the *Tutsi*-led army also took power in Burundi. As a result, ethnic *Hutu* fled because of the insecurity. This flood of refugees continued relentlessly so that in 1996 the United Nations High Commissioner for Refugees (UNHCR) spoke of more than 1.2 million refugees crowded in camps across the western borders of Rwanda and Burundi. Their plight was appalling because they were not allowed to settle permanently. In many camps permanent schools and hospitals were forbidden. The corruption of the Zaïrean army made it easy for those who wanted to prepare a reconquest to obtain weapons and even to launch commando operations into Rwanda and Burundi. The UNHCR was not able to disarm the militants. Neither were the Zaïrean army nor the international community able to solve the problem. The time bomb was ticking, and hundreds of thousands of innocent civilians were caught between hammer and anvil.

---

[1] *La Vie*, 2722 (October 30, 1997), 10.

The Archbishop

One man saw clearly what was happening and spoke out repeatedly. *Mzee*[2] Christophe Munzihirwa Mwene Ngabo was born at Burhale, not far from Bukavu, in 1926. He was ordained a priest in 1958. He joined the Jesuits in 1965, and became superior of their province of Central Africa (Zaïre, Rwanda and Burundi) in 1980. In 1986 he became a bishop, and in 1994 was appointed archbishop of Bukavu. He immediately took a courageous stand against the injustices in the Great Lakes region. On August 27, 1992, he noted in his journal this quotation from Berdiaeff [Berdyayev]: "The only elevated place in this world's hierarchy is to be crucified for the truth."

The following are extracts of Mgr. Munzihirwa's interventions:[3]

➢ On July 24, 1994, Mgr. Munzihirwa spoke openly against the way the population of Bukavu had plundered the houses left empty in Cyangugu on the other side of the border, and had then sold these goods openly in Bukavu town. He denounced the harassment of Rwandan refugees by Zaïrean soldiers at the border-posts.

➢ On July 31, 1994, he protested the theft of vehicles from Rwandan refugees by Zaïrean soldiers. He reacted against the unwillingness of the *HCR* to bring permanent assistance to the refugees (some were saying "let those *Hutu* murderers die!"), and asked the international community to help bring about a movement of reconciliation of all Rwandans.

➢ On August 2, 1994, he wrote a letter to Mr. Boutros Boutros-Ghali, entitled *"Non-assistance to Rwandan refugees in danger of death in Bukavu, Zaïre."*

➢ On August 3, 1994, Mgr. Munzihirwa wrote a five page manifesto highlighting the motivations behind the violence and hypocrisy in Rwanda and Burundi: an attempt to gain absolute power while ordinary people were left as victims.

➢ On August 7, 1994, he wrote to president François Mitterand, telling him of the necessity to postpone the withdrawal of French troops (*Opération Turquoise*) from the security zones in Rwanda, lest thousands of frightened civilians storm across the border.

➢ On September 8, 1994, he spoke against arbitrary imprisonment and other retaliation against the *Hutu* population in Rwanda and the victimization of refugees by the Zaïrean army in Bukavu.

---

[2] *Mzee* is a Swahili honorific meaning *elder.*

[3] Philippe de Dordolot, *"Les réfugiés rwandais à Bukavu au Zaïre: de nouveau Palestiniens?"* (Paris: L'Harmattan, 1996).

- On September 19, 1994, he spoke again to a representative of a humanitarian organization (*Misereor*) about the need to prepare the necessary preconditions for the return of Rwandan refugees – the establishment of the rule of law in Rwanda.

- On January 16, 1995, Mgr. Munzihirwa wrote to Cardinal Daneels, President of *Pax Christi*, and to the President of the Justice and Peace commission in France, to explain that pressure should be brought to bear on the regime in Kigali, so that they would begin to accept a negotiated settlement with their fellow citizens, refugees in Zaïre, thus making their return possible.

- On April 22, 1995, at Kibeho, in the zone previously protected by *Opération Turquoise,* a camp of displaced people was attacked by the *FPR* army. Thousands of civilians – men, women and children – who had nowhere to take refuge, were killed. Humanitarian groups were witnesses. One witness, a member of *MINUAR*, saw 4,054 bodies buried in a mass grave.[4]

- On April 28, 1995, Munzihirwa spoke of the resistance movement growing among *Hutu* refugees. He saw this as the inevitable consequence of a gradual extermination of *Hutu* militants and innocent civilians in Rwanda. There were even commando attacks of *FPR* soldiers in refugee camps in Zaïre. He said: "The international community seems to accept that an armed minority, simply to ensure that it stays in power, can with impunity exterminate an unarmed majority." And he denounced those who supply the weapons in this war, mentioning in particular the supply of armaments and military personnel by president Museveni of Uganda to the *Tutsi* armies in Rwanda and Burundi.

- On May 15, 1995, he wrote another memorandum to Boutros Boutros-Ghali and to the President of the European Commission. Once again he denounced the merciless repression perpetrated by the regime in Kigali, and explained how this exacerbated the resistance movement. He appealed for outside intervention to foster an attitude of dialogue between the military power in Kigali and representatives of the *Hutu* refugees packed along the eastern border of Zaïre. He warned of the danger of "implosion" in the region if nothing were done.

- On October 6, 1995, Mgr. Munzihirwa wrote to the United Nations High Commissioner for Refugees [UNHCR], to explain that the repatriation of the refugees could not be forced, and that the pretense of good will on the part of the regime in Kigali was belied by the facts: repeated massacres, and incarceration awaiting any refugees who came back.

---

[4] *Médecins Sans Frontières*, 37, Juin 1995.

The Martyr

And so the archbishop continued to speak out fearlessly in favor of dialogue as the only true foundation of a lasting peace. On September 27, 1996, he was still insisting on the need to resolve differences through dialogue rather than through exclusion. And on October 19, 1996, on the opening of the new academic year at the University of Bukavu, he said: "A university is grounded on an attitude of dialogue between diverse ethnic groups. Our happiness should be to see all the ethnic groups of the Great Lakes region come together as brothers (and sisters) and become richer through this continuous dialogue."

In 1996 Paul Kagame informed the American authorities and probably other countries also that he was prepared to act unilaterally to put an end to the threat coming from the refugees in Zaïre if the international community could not intervene.[5]

Using as bridgehead a group of *Tutsi* immigrants south of Uvira in Zaïre, called the *banyamulenge*, the campaign spread rapidly. On October 29, 1996, the town of Bukavu was attacked by *Tutsi* soldiers (*banyamulenge*, Rwandaris, Burundians and Ugandans). In town, all those in authority had fled. People considered Mgr. Munzihirwa the last sentinel of Bukavu. At 5.55 p.m. he had finished a meeting with a committee to see how people – now beginning to panic – could be calmed down. As he drove back home, he was stopped by a group of soldiers coming from the border. His army escort was killed. Munzihirwa said he was the archbishop, holding his cross in his hand. He was led aside. The soldiers sent a radio message for their orders. Then they shot him once in the back of the head.

His body stayed there until the afternoon of the following day, because the town was gripped by fear. Anything that moved was being shot at. When some priests were able to recover his body, they used the wood of church benches to put together a makeshift coffin. The next day a few people took the risk of moving out and attended a very simple burial ceremony. This is how this fearless spokesman of justice, truth and dialogue died. Four years previously he had written in his diary: "Life, said a philosopher, is like a sentence, the meaning of which can only be understood when the last word has been said."

The Choir

The Missionary Sisters of Our Lady of Africa have for many years had a house in Kadutu, the shantytown of Bukavu. Their numbers have diminished,

[5] *La Vie*, ibid.

and they have a large chapel which they made available for people of the neighborhood to assemble for Sunday Eucharist. It became the favorite place for the youth of the area, and they formed a choir which rapidly gained a reputation. It was named the "Lavigerie Choir."

Mgr. Munzihirwa used to come to talk to the young people practically every Sunday at the end of their liturgy. He shared with them his concern for peace and justice and his anxiety about the deteriorating situation in the area and in town. In response to the message of the archbishop, the young people composed songs which they subsequently would put together in cassettes to be put on sale. These songs echo the concerns of the archbishop and illustrate the way in which his message was assimilated by the youth. Their first cassette was made in 1995 and was entitled *Mass for Unity*. It gives their own Christian response to the ethnic conflict and division that was developing around them.

During 1996 the situation was building up to a major conflagration. Mgr. Munzihirwa shared his deep foreboding with the youth of the chapel in Kadutu. In solidarity and response, they started composing a series of songs on the theme of peace. Then war broke out and Mgr. Munzihirwa was assassinated.

The young people were shattered. At the height of the attack many of them fled the town. But after some weeks, in November 1996, they began to return. The members of the choir met again and shared their grief. They felt they had to put into words and music their profoundest thoughts and feelings about all that had happened. First, they gathered the songs about peace, and to them they added some of their archbishop's words, which one of them had recorded from his radio messages. This cassette was entitled *The Peace You Need*. Here are some extracts of the lyrics: *Rights are trampled underfoot / People are oppressed / We hear the shouts of the downtrodden / Together let us say NO to violence, NO to suspicion, NO to tribalism ...*

As they worked on this cassette they became more deeply aware of the relevance and impact of the words and testimony of their archbishop. Living, as they were, under foreign occupation falsely presented as a liberation, they became conscious of the hypocrisy and the duplicity which their archbishop had been denouncing. They began to understand that the death of their dear Christophe was no pointless accident. They now saw clearly that this "monument of peace" could not have remained standing while the merciless massacre of hundreds of thousands of refugees was being perpetrated. They understood only too well that the "voice speaking on behalf on the voiceless" had to be silenced so that the systematic elimination of people who were a potential danger to those clinging to power could be done discreetly and unobtrusively.

They became fully conscious of the fact that their archbishop had died as a martyr for the truth.

This final message – the death of their friend – was extremely rich and powerful. In a matter of a few short weeks they reacted the only way they could. They composed songs to cry out their grief, to state their faith, and to proclaim their attachment to the person of Christophe and his message. They sang their admiration for his commitment and his courage up to death, and their own willingness to tread the same path. They had no doubt that he was a martyr: a witness to the truth of the Gospel even to the final sacrifice of his life. The combination of words and music in this new cassette entitled *Machosi ni mengi (Tears A-Plenty)* is extremely moving. The words perpetuate in their own way the commitment of Archbishop Munzihirwa. Here are some more extracts:

> *They have shut our mouth. We have no one to speak for us. We have lost the servant of peace. They told me he had died; I wasn't in the least surprised; it's the way of the Christians.*

> *If Christophe was gunned down, maybe I'll be bombed .... But I must tell the truth; truth is stronger than everything.*

> *Warmongers, have pity! Stop the war! The monument of peace lay on the ground, on the road of Nyawera. Yet he had no weapons ... only his rosary. He was alone against an army. He died because he told the torturers: stop making tears flow.*

> *I am tired ... I am tired of this ungrateful world.*

> *When the stars and the sun are gathered in one place ... I'll see Christophe, the great martyr, with his wise old smile ... I'll see old [Mzee] Christophe in heaven.*

> *Christophe may have been killed, but truth has not been killed!*

Inculturation and Contextualization

The circumstances experienced by the people of Bukavu during the last three years were a radical challenge. Rampant corruption had already rendered the social and moral fabric weak and fragile. Many people lived on the verge of total poverty; they could barely survive. Law and order had practically disappeared.

Then this already densely populated area was invaded by hordes of refugees of all kinds, some bitterly opposed to others, some rich and powerful, some armed, many in a most desperate state. To make matters worse, international agents came in with big money (i.e. compared with the means of

151

ordinary people), with opportunities for well-paid jobs, and willing to pay good rents for houses. Prices of goods shot up. The mighty dollar reigned. Some citizens responded to the opportunity and became rich overnight. The weakest were left aside and forgotten, or used and exploited. A multitude of suffering humanity vegetated in camps while the international community failed – or refused – to intervene and settle the dispute or determine a course of action.

The great majority of people in Bukavu are Christians; more than half of them Catholics. The immediate and burning question for them was: what is the relevance of the Gospel of Jesus Christ in our present situation? For many Christians, especially the evangelicals, their faith became a means of escape: they found relief in religious singing and prayers for healing, surviving their present trials by means of their hope for some later retribution or a better world.

Archbishop Munzihirwa was not one of those. Publicly and explicitly he took a stand to indicate that the message of Christ has a relevance that penetrates the present uncertainty and conflict to its depths. For the people of Bukavu, theirs had become a culture of social conflict and unrest, of ethnic hatred, of injustice and *anomie*. There was no limit to what some people would do for the sake of survival; selfishness was the rule, the absolute necessity. Might was right: that was unquestioned and unquestionable. But there was another voice: *Mzee* Christophe proclaimed loud and clear that the duty of a Christian is to speak the truth, to denounce evil, and to foster dialogue with untiring effort. He preached by word and example, in moments opportune and importune.

It is my contention that the attitude of *Mzee* Munzihirwa illustrates one of the correct ways of inculturating the Gospel message. The response of the "Lavigerie Choir" was an extension of this way. The archbishop's life, death and legacy are a contextual response, a convergence of theory and practice or theology and life. His approach, both personally and in terms of his ability to inspire others, was to use the challenge of actual circumstances as a summons to existential Christian living.

Today many parts of Africa are in a state of turmoil. This is sometimes caused, and always accompanied by rapid cultural change. One might speak of a progressive loss of culture – de-culturation – leading to cultural uncertainty and to eclecticism or syncretism. Grafting the Gospel onto dying cultures is not an appropriate response.[6] The explicit Gospel teaching can become an important element, a beneficial ferment in the reconstruction of a new social

[6] See the chapter by A. C. Edwards, in this volume.

152

fabric. But that is a long-range prospect. Meanwhile we must *do* inculturation *now*. *Now* simply does not permit us to wait for things to settle down. *Now* cannot justify a moratorium on inculturation. *Now* means that in the midst of tensions and conflicts we must be living our faith. Inculturation is indeed a messy business, if it is pursued in such circumstances. As this chapter illustrates, it is also a dangerous business. But we cannot escape social and political involvement. It is our duty to engage with reality, filled with conviction and determination.

So let us not forget the "Lavigerie Choir." It is, so to speak, the fertile soil in which the message of the old archbishop has taken root and flourished. The cassettes are the fruit of *Mzee* Munzihirwa's sacrifice. This illustrates the fact that inculturation and contextualization of the faith are already happening, in numerous places and in unexpected ways. Some enlightened members of the official church may proclaim the message in formal terms. Some may identify formal channels through which inculturation is to be guided. But the implementation is being done – must be done, and in the final analysis can only be done – by ordinary Christians. This is not to drive a wedge between the official church and ordinary people, but simply to acknowledge reality. Sometimes people do operate *outside* the official church structures; and sometimes circumstances are unprecedented and not covered by official rules and texts. In this respect, subsequent events surrounding the activities of the "Lavigerie Choir" are rather enlightening, and a brief account may serve as an appropriate conclusion.

Conclusion

During 1997, people in Bukavu learned to live under occupation. The open warfare was over but the firm foundation for peace was as elusive as ever. The "Lavigerie Choir" presented some concerts and performed their repertoire of songs on various occasions. However, the youth and the choir no longer met on Sundays in the sisters' chapel; they were invited to join the services at the parish church. The choir now animates one of the parish Masses on Sunday afternoon. The group has been reintegrated into the general framework of the parish. They have also lost much of their independence and creativity. Where will they find the motivation to write new songs?

The figure of *Mzee* Munzihirwa is venerated. His memory is cherished. People have no doubt but that he died a martyr's death. His courage is admired. On October 29, 1997 – the anniversary of his death – they gathered in great numbers in the cathedral. Yet to some extent, his voice has been effectively silenced. Another message has got through also: that it is extremely dangerous to dissent openly.

Nevertheless: committed Christians know now that the only answer to the impasse in which they find themselves is truth, dialogue, tolerance and reconciliation. They know this is the only firm foundation on which justice and true peace can be built. They continue to hope. And they have begun to speak out. On January 1, 1998, the cathedral of Bukavu was packed once again on the occasion of a Mass for Peace. At the end of the ceremony two female university students, members of the "Lavigerie Choir," presented a very moving song which portrayed the injustices and miseries which people still have to undergo; and they prayed for God's love to enter all hearts that together we may all construct peace. Then three women, all of whom are mothers, made a very explicit declaration against the continuing culture of violence, the lack of respect for life, the killing and the intimidation, the injustices which thrive in neighboring countries and overflow in the region, and the exploitation of children, soldiers, and so on. They took a solemn pledge to direct all their energies to combat such evils during the New Year, and to work for peace and reconciliation.

Truly, through these dark days and terrible experiences, the Gospel message has shown its power to penetrate some people's lives more deeply. It is becoming inculturated in the present. It has been successfully contextualized through the life and death of *Mzee* Christophe Munzihirwa.

The Lyrics

Though there are several cassettes of songs by the "Lavigerie Choir," many readers of this book will be unable to obtain them. Since the lyrics are so powerful, some of them are included here, both as a testimony to *Mzee* Munzihirwa and the choir, and by way of example and encouragement to those who might be inspired to take up the challenge.

Machosi ni mengi: Tears A-Plenty

Yee! Tears a-plenty. Mountains and sky fell on us. Why, we can't breathe anymore.
They have already shut our mouth. We have no one to speak for us.
We have lost the servant of peace. Why, we don't know what to do.
Yes, indeed, I cry. Sadness, yee! Tears a-plenty.

I saw an old man passing. He was wearing the clothes of a watchman.
They told me, "hey, it's the bishop. His name is Christophe Munzihirwa."
What kind of bishop would humble himself, to the extent of living like a poor person?
Let me cry. Sadness, yee! Tears a-plenty.

They told me that he had died. I wasn't in the least surprised.
It's their rule, the real Christians: to give themselves up, like their own Jesus.
If you carry your cross up to Golgotha, it's normal you'll rise again like their Jesus.
I have great faith in that Christophe ... he is alive in front of his Jesus.

La verité est plus forte: Truth is stronger

In the time of Christ, the cross gave birth to the resurrection.
For the first Christians, persecution strengthened the church.
In my time I was lucky to see the blood of a just man,
The death of a martyr is fertility for the church.

The servant is never greater than the master.
If Jesus was crucified, if St. Paul was beheaded,
If Kizito was burned, Anuarité was speared through,
If Bakanja was tortured, Christophe was gunned down –
Perhaps I will be bombed, but I must tell the truth.

Like Christophe, I'll not be afraid. Torturers the world over
Have no power over me, because truth is stronger than everything.
Because if all the crosses and all the armies
Could not intimidate our precursors – Jesus, Luther King, Romero –
Or even old Christophe, yes! Truth is stronger than everything.

Truth gives birth to love, and love gives birth to peace,
And peace gives birth to joy. Thank you, thank you, thank you, Christophe!

Niende wapi: Where should I go?

REFRAIN: Where should I go again, Lord? Your words are sweet.
Truly I have proclaimed them. I have given myself to you.

I have given you my youth and I served the Gospel; then you sent me to the fire.
I tried to quench it; then you sent me to war. There I have brought peace.

REFRAIN

I have given you my old age when I carried the Gospel; then you sent me to Kasongo.
I have brought joy there; then you sent me to Bukavu. I have tried to be their
servant.

REFRAIN

O Lord! I have completed your work. I have given you my life;
to you my Lord and God.
O Lord! I have come to do your will. I will give you my life;
to you my Lord and God.

REFRAIN

Kwa mfano wa Yesu: By Jesus' example

REFRAIN: By the example of Jesus you have carried the Cross.
You have shed your blood, Christophe, for the sake of those you loved.

You were an old man without strength; you suffered illnesses of all kinds.
But you have done your work well so that we may find happiness.

REFRAIN

You reproached the wrongdoers without the least discrimination.
Neither did you fear any one. You are an example of righteousness.

REFRAIN

Elder Munzihirwa, teach us wisdom; you, elder of elders, teach us wisdom.
Elder of truth, may we be witnesses. Witnesses of peace, may we be witnesses.
Example for Christians, teach us the Gospel.
You, Christian in truth, teach us the Gospel.
Bishop in poverty, may the priests be many.
You, perfect priest, may the priests be many.
Disciple of Jesus, may peace reign. Victor of Nyawera, may peace reign.

Disons non: Let us say no!

When discord comes, fears hunt people down.
We hear the rumbles of war, the shouts of the downtrodden.
Those who keep the peace have turned it into plundering, theft, rape and murder.
Right is trampled underfoot; the people are oppressed; right belongs to the mightiest.

Yet it is close by, that peace that always blossoms,
Waiting for its harvesters, the youth of the world.
May everything be born anew, weapons be thrown away.
May the day of liberation come.

Let us awaken and search for peace. Every person is a sacred story.
This is possible if the youth stands up like one, to build up again,
So that the coming years may be rich in peace and joy,
Peaceful for all. Together, let us say no to violence.

QUESTIONS

1. With this chapter as an example, can you identify social/political/religious realities in a culture familiar to you, that stimulate a Christian response in justice?

2. Song and dance are quintessential aspects of African experience. Does the use of song depicted in this chapter surprise you? Can you imagine approaching inculturation through the media of song and dance? Discuss this, and give examples you know.

3. What do you think about the effectiveness of the songs cited at the end of this chapter? Using the lyrics and the broader context of the chapter, is it possible to relate "spontaneous inculturation" to the forms of inculturation discussed in Chapter One?

4. One sad reflection in this chapter concerns the effect of the movement of the *Lavigerie Choir* from the sisters' convent to the parish church. It appears that this move served to "domesticate" the choir: at least its creativity was seriously restrained. What lesson does this suggest to you as you ponder appropriate methods of inculturation?

5. The lyrics of the songs appeal to the depths of one's soul and speak a language that transcends many of the other sentiments in this book. Do you agree? How do you respond to this observation?

CHAPTER TEN

RELIGIOUS PROFESSION RITES AS BAROMETERS –
IGBO, NIGERIA

Joan F. Burke, S.N.D.-N.

The effects of inculturation must reach every part of life. The following research-in-progress report on Nigeria and beyond looks at the shape of religious profession in women's communities. For those interested in the possibilities of inculturating liturgies other than the Roman Rite of the Mass, and for anyone working in a context other than a conventional parish, this offers many practical indications of what might be done.

Introduction

African women religious are key agents of inculturation in today's church. Significant, in my mind, is that they are not normally long removed from their local environments. By contrast, men who aspire to the clerical state spend long years in insulated seminaries following a very regimented, institutional life with great emphasis on the mastery of "Western book knowledge." Both for this reason and because their work normally brings them into closer association with ordinary people, I place great stock in African women religious as much more responsive agents for the inculturation of the church at the base. Their ears and hearts are close to the *sensus fidelium*.

Bediako wrote: "... following the Christianization of African tradition [John Mbiti *et al.*], African Christianity must [now] achieve an *Africanization* of its Christian experience, and this latter may prove to be the more demanding task."[1] [my emphasis] For African Christians, this is the heart of the matter today. Religious profession rites are a particularly relevant topic in this context: they foreground the essential importance of African Christians searching to express their experience of their faith in local categories. Such rites should demonstrate that Christianity is actually being appropriated in African terms, and show how a significant group of Christians is understanding and trying to communicate the meaning of their faith to their fellow Africans.

In this chapter I will describe efforts of African women religious to articulate the meaning of religious life in local categories which provide evi-

---

[1] Kwame Bediako, *Christianity in Africa: The Renewal of a Non-Western Religion* (Maryknoll, NY: Orbis Books, 1995).

dence that the received institution has been appropriated (e.g., image of the church as the "Family of God"). This is a report on research-in-progress rather than a finished study. Perhaps it will stimulate other women religious – in Africa and beyond – to examine how profession rites might serve the People of God as a pedagogy of the vows and religious life.

Part One: Religious Life in Africa

A paper given by the renowned Belgian missiologist Pierre Charles at the *Louvain Missiology Week* in 1950 is enlightening. The Jesuit scholar begins by tracing in an illuminating way the reasons why the Catholic church until relatively recently did not regard women as being either worthy or competent to serve as missionaries. Then Charles documents what he calls *la missiologie antiféministe,* which existed until the end of the nineteenth century. First he gives a resumé of the arguments against women missionaries put forth in 1682 by Cardinal Laurent Brancati, a former Prefect of Studies (i.e., Director) at the College of Propaganda in Rome:

> The [missionaries'] unique function is to preach the Word of God and his commandment; that is why they are sent, *missi* ... Who then can be a missionary? The reply comes as an obvious axiom: none but men. All women are excluded from this function and will never be able to aspire to it ... And the author reaches the conclusion by way of a very decisive syllogism: the work of the missionary is to preach, and preaching is a work of wisdom. Now, according to Aristotle, *sapientia non viget communiter in mulieribus*: wisdom is not commonly found in women. The consequence is clear to the author. He reinforces it, moreover, by an appeal to the celebrated text of St. Paul, on women who must keep quiet in church; ... [in spite of its meaning] something quite different.[2]

The missiologist points out that Brancati's position was not new, but an argument for what was the correct missionary practice. Even during the great expansion of missionary activity in the sixteenth and seventeenth centuries, there were no women missionaries. During that period, the women religious who did go to Canada (Ursulines) and Ecuador were all members of cloistered monasteries – and remained so even in the New World. In Quito, Ecuador, there was apparently one monastery enclosing eight hundred Spanish nuns. Pierre Charles observes ironically, "There is the whole country still to be converted, but the enclosure is absolute and not one of these vocations is used

---

[2] Pierre Charles, "Missiologie antiféministe," in *Le rôle de la femme dans les missions: rapports et compte rendu de la XXe Semaine de Missiologie de Louvain 1950* (Bruxelles: Ed. Universelle/Paris: Desclée de Brouwer, 1951), 20-21.

in the work of the mission. That is reserved exclusively for men."[3] The first invitation to women religious to take an active part in Africa came not from the church but from the French government.

Following the French Revolution, there developed in Europe and especially in France over six hundred new religious orders of men and of women founded for specific kinds of socially oriented works, such as teaching and nursing.[4] In contrast to the older monastic orders which were cloistered and dedicated entirely to prayer and contemplation, these religious congregations were frequently called active or apostolic because of the type of work they undertook. Charles recounts that the French government under the Restoration, seeing the works of these newer congregations, asked the foundress of the Sisters of St. Joseph of Cluny, Anne-Marie Javouhey (1779-1851), to send some of her Sisters "to assure the education of the daughters of the *colons* (colonials), at Saint-Louis in Sénégal and in the French possession of Guiana."[5] Accepting the invitation, she sent a group to Sénégal in 1819; she herself worked there from 1822-1824. In 1828 she accompanied the first Sisters going to French Guiana where they set up a self-supporting colony of enfranchised slaves. Her efforts were not at all appreciated by the churchmen of her time. Charles comments:

> When she founded there [French Guiana] her great black institution ... which was a huge success, the objections came thick and fast. It's inconceivable, people said, that there isn't a man at the head of this enterprise: slanderous accusations and lampoons rained upon her; and when she was boarding ship to return to Europe, the clergy unanimously refused her not only Holy Communion but even absolution. Her crime was to have wanted to be a missionary to the blacks. This presumptuousness seemed to merit a punishment that is not inflicted even on those condemned to die.[6]

At the end of the nineteenth century, when the Jesuits accepted the invitation of King Leopold II of Belgium, to evangelize the Lower Congo, they had believed from the outset that it was essential for women religious to accompany them and to work with the local women and children. This was due in no small measure to their assessment of why the Jesuits and the early Capuchin missioners in the Ancient Kingdom of the Kongo had failed in the

---

[3] *Op. cit.,* 22.

[4] Lawrence Cada et. al., *Shaping the Coming Age of Religious Life* (New York, NY: Seabury, 1979), 11-50; Maurice Monnette, *Kindred Spirits: Bonding of Laity and Religious* (Kansas City, MO: Sheed and Ward, 1987), 38.

[5] Charles, *ibid.*

[6] Charles, *op.cit.,* 22-23.

first evangelization of the region, which began in the mid-sixteenth century. The founder of the Jesuit mission at Kimwenza wrote in July 1893:

> Without [women religious], without the education of the young black girls, the conversion of the Congolese families is absolutely impossible. It is in great part the lack of women religious for the education of the black girls that has for so long hindered and rendered sterile the work of our former missionaries of old in the savage regions of Portuguese Congo.[7]

This position was argued at length in an article, "L'Apostolat des Sœurs dans les Missions Etrangères" published in the Jesuit mission magazine:

> If the progress of religion among the savage tribes and pagan nations has been sometimes so slow and painful, it is to the absence of women religious – who are like the teachers sent by providence for a good half of the human race – that these checks and delays can be attributed. Thus in the earlier Portuguese Congo of olden days, neither in San Salvador nor in San Paulo de Louanda, nor anywhere else, was there anybody to take care of the instruction of the Christian women, that great component of moral growth and civilisation. The poor negresses stagnated in the most abject ignorance and they [the missionaries] never succeeded in forming truly Christian families nor native populations that were fundamentally religious and moral.[8]

After a time, young African women wanted to join the sisters in their work. Pope Pius XI encouraged European Orders and Congregations to found local religious communities. In 1926 he wrote in the encyclical *Rerum Ecclesiae*:

> ... if there are any natives desirous of joining the older congregations, it certainly would not be right to discourage them or to impede them from joining. ... Still, let them ponder seriously and prayerfully the question whether it might not be more expedient to found new congregations such as may answer better the genius and character of the natives, and be more in keeping with the needs and spirit of the country.[9]

At the first plenary session of the Episcopal Conference of the Belgian Congo and Rwanda-Burundi in 1932, the bishops stated clearly their preference that local women be encouraged to join African diocesan congregations rather than international ones.[10] After World War II, they gave permission for

---

[7] Emiel van Hencxthoven, in *Précis Historiques: Bulletin mensuel des Missions Belges de la Compagnie de Jésus* (1893), 509.

[8] Victor Baesten, in *Précis Historiques* (1894), 200.

[9] Raymond Hickey, *Modern Missionary Documents and Africa* (Dublin: Dominican Publications, 1982), 65.

[10] *La vie religieuse au Zaïre* [Colloque de Kinshasa, 15-21 août, 1979] (Pro Mundi Vita Dossier Afrique 14, Bruxelles: Pro Mundi Vita, 1980).

the women themselves to choose whichever congregation they preferred to enter. By 1955 there were 870 African Sisters in the three Belgian colonies.[11] Most were members of diocesan congregations. Statistics given in the *Pro Mundi Vita* study done in 1980 give the following picture of the development of congregations in Congo-Kinshasa:

before 1930:	1 congregation founded
1930-45:	13 congregations founded
1945-60:	3 congregations
1960-75:	7 congregations[12]

I estimate that the development across Africa was proportionate in the time periods given. The Missionary Sisters of Our Lady of Africa – known at the time as the White Sisters – were particularly instrumental in helping to found numerous African congregations. The same report states that 2,164 of the 4,220 Catholic women religious working in the then Zaïre in 1979 were Africans, that is 51.2%.[13] By 1994 according to the Catholic Secretariat in Lagos, Nigeria, the number of women religious in Africa was 47,572.

It is clear that women religious are a formidable force in the church of Africa today. Besides their initial work in the establishment of the basic infrastructure and outreach to women and children, they continue to minister to the educational, health, development and pastoral needs of hundreds of thousands on the continent; in many cases, they minister impartially to Christians and non-Christians. They are far more ubiquitous than clerics. More frequently they are found at the grassroots – truly immersed in the daily realities of their people.

Part Two: Profession Rites as Ritual

Methodology Itself as a "Way In"

In the process of inculturation, one thing strikes me as being of fundamental importance: the effort expended by the believing community as it tries to bring to consciousness and name its own experience of the treasure of the Word. Every community receives the treasure in an earthen vessel, made from someone else's clay (cf. 2 Cor 4:7). Inevitably, the message must first be carried in the particular form and expression of its bearers. But as the message is

---

[11] M. Norberta, "La formation des sœurs indigènes en Afrique," *Bulletin de l'Union Missionnaire du Clergé* 35 (1955), 108-116.

[12] *La vie religieuse*, 8.

[13] *Op. cit.*, 7.

internalized and lived, the new bearers must develop their own appropriate forms and expressions. It is crucial that they – the recipients – reflect on their own understanding of the Gospel message and develop appropriate responses to it. As they do so, new insights will become available for sharing with other communities of believers. This in turn produces the very stuff of further inculturation among sister-churches. And in that ensuing, on-going dialogue, all the People of God can be drawn into what St. Paul calls "the breadth and the length, the height and the depth" of the marvels of God's love revealed in Jesus.

Inculturation of Profession Rites

The ritual of the public profession of vows and incorporation into a religious congregation provides a stimulus for the new member to reflect on the *word* (vow formula in the vernacular) as an expression of the *meaning* of religious life. Further, as a public ceremony, it affords an opportunity for the religious to share with the faithful of the local church a "pedagogy of religious life." How African women religious see, understand, and express themselves in terms understandable in the local cultural context might be seen as a barometer of inculturation in different parts of Africa.

Until relatively recently, many persistent difficulties inhibited the inculturation of rites of religious profession. First, the canonical formation given to the aspiring religious was almost entirely in a foreign language, and actually embedded in foreign categories. This would also have been true of the various models of the actual expression of religious life (models of social relationships, of authority and group decision-making, conflict resolution and so on). Second, religious life – and indeed Christianity itself – was generally presented more as an *institution* than as a *movement*.[14] And thirdly, in my view, there has been an overemphasis, historically, on the vows of poverty, chastity and obedience as summarizing the meaning of religious life. A consequent effort to translate the words of these three vows *literally* has obscured rather than revealed the heart-meaning of religious life. This does not seem too problematic in the case of obedience. However, a literal translation of the words *poverty* and *chastity* has little or no positive value in the African socio-religious context.

[14] Sandra Schneiders, *New Wineskins: Re-imagining Religious Life Today* (New York: Paulist Press, 1986), chapter 2; David Bosch, *Transforming Mission: Paradigm Shifts in the Theology of Mission* (Maryknoll, NY: Orbis Books, 1991), 41-43, 50-53.

Contemporary Interest in Profession Rites

Since the widely-quoted declaration of Paul VI at Kampala in 1969, the general attitude of the official church has not only shown itself more open to cultural expressions of Christianity, but has actually encouraged and promoted efforts at inculturation. At the All Africa Symposium of the Catholic hierarchy the Pontiff had told the gathered bishops:

> The expression [of the one faith], that is, the language and mode of manifesting it, may be manifold. Hence, it may be original, suited to the tongue, the style, the character, the genius, and the culture, of the one who professes this one faith. From this point of view, a certain pluralism is not only legitimate, but desirable. An adaptation of the Christian life in the fields of pastoral, ritual, didactic and spiritual activities, is not only possible, it is even favored by the Church. The liturgical renewal is a living example of this. And in this sense you may, and you must, have an African Christianity. Indeed you possess human values and characteristic forms of culture which can rise up to perfection such as to find in Christianity, and for Christianity, a true superior fullness, and prove to be capable of a richness of expression all its own, and genuinely African.[15]

Another significant factor has contributed to the attitudes of African religious themselves: social change may have helped them appear less defensive of their chosen lifestyle and more assertive in defining themselves. Many people have now had a long-time association with women religious. Parents and families, as well as catechists and teachers who work with sisters, have often been asked to explain the life of women religious in the church. Increasingly then, religious themselves are becoming more open to what might be described as existing latent models of and for religious life and leadership among their people. An example of this would be the *Ma Ndona* among the Kongo people in Lower Congo-Kinshasa. She is the female counterpart of the clan chief, and one of her prerogatives and responsibilities is to foster harmony and reconciliation.[16] Another example is illustrated by persons consecrated to shrines of divinities in Central and Eastern Nigeria.

But religious congregations in Africa are themselves quite evidently maturing, as well as increasingly coming into contact with other local churches and different cultures. Both of these factors stimulate some of the members at least, to clarify their particular way of understanding religious life. In certain congregations, members are encouraged to write their own vow formulas: this

---

[15] Quoted in Hickey, *op. cit.,* 203-204.

[16] Joan F. Burke, "These Catholic Sisters Are All *Mamas!*," in F. Bowie, D. Kirkwood, S. Ardener (eds), *Women and Missions: Past and Present,* (Oxford: Berg, 1993), 251-266.

challenges many to actually attempt to articulate their own understanding of religious life. The current practice in Nigeria is that the formula at First Profession is normally in English, while the vernacular is increasingly being used for the rite of Final Profession. There has also been a theological tendency in recent years to put an increased emphasis on Christians reflecting on their concrete experience. This appears to have affected sisters and the way in which they are re-examining the traditional explanations of their lives as religious.

Rites of Final Profession

Efforts are beginning to be made to inculturate the rite and to find ways of making it more meaningful to the local church as well as to the particular community. However, this is not yet a general practice; nationally, the church in Nigeria is not over-keen on the practical fostering of inculturation.

Recently, over the course of a year, I carried out a preliminary survey of profession rituals used by ten different congregations of women religious.[17] Much more work still needs to be done, to foster and document the work on profession rites. At this juncture, the following factors seem to me to be especially significant:

➤ the role and involvement of the parents and family;
➤ the local models being drawn upon (e.g., marriage rites; dedication of persons to shrines of divinities; initiation rites);
➤ the symbols employed, and the explanations offered (whether they are local symbols or imported);
➤ the role and content of the commentary;
➤ the involvement of other members of the religious community (for purposes of ratification, covenanting, welcoming new members, and so on);
➤ the use of the local language, particularly in the actual vow formula (when the formula is composed by the person professing vows, is there a vernacular text and a *literal translation in English?*).

Below is a summary of my findings relative to rituals of the profession of final vows.

Common elements: Gifts are presented to the newly professed. During the ritual itself, after the profession of vows, all finally professed sisters of the

---

[17] Sisters of the Sacred Heart, Benin City (SSH); Sisters of the Holy Child Jesus (SHCJ); Daughters of the Holy Trinity, Kumasi (FST); Sisters of the Immaculate Heart (IHM); Sisters of Notre Dame de Namur (SND); Missionary Sisters of the Holy Rosary (MSHR); Sisters of Our Lady of Fatima, Jos (OLF); Religious Sisters of Charity (RSC); Dominican Sisters, Sokoto (OP); Little Sisters of Jesus (LSJ). All information refers to Nigeria.

congregation present come forward and pronounce an act of covenant over the sister and then embrace her as a sign of welcome. Parents are invited to express their agreement, which is sometimes done by their praying blessing on their daughter. A big reception follows at which the sister may be presented with traditional gifts. In some areas of Nigeria (and also in Congo-Kinshasa), the finally professed woman religious is henceforth addressed as *Mother*.

Distinctive features: Sisters are escorted into church by groups of small dancing girls (as an 'age set' would do for their mate in accompanying her to the house of her husband), amidst shouts and songs of joy (SSH). During the processional, young girls in traditional attire carry the rings on a cushion (FST). Parents offer to their daughters the following: a Bible symbolising their missionary call; a piece of cloth and some slippers for the journey they are embarking upon (FST). Sisters are encouraged to pronounce their vows in their mother tongue (FST; OLF; SND; IHM). Those who will be professed spend three months in a designated place which serves as a retreat center, preparing themselves in a "tertianship" - similar to the isolation of an *Igbo* "fattening hut" for women before marriage (IHM). Sisters prostrate themselves during the Litany of the Saints, which is adapted to include their own patrons (IHM). The sister herself composes her own vow formula in keeping with guidelines of the congregation (SND). After professing vows, sisters then face the congregation and do their "praise dance" (MSHR).

What is particularly significant is that the dominant local model on which profession rites are based is that of marriage. Interestingly though, the emphasis is not on the spousal relationship – though this is naturally present – but on the person's having henceforth a changed relationship with her family and likewise the family with their daughter's religious community. In the rituals there is also the suggestion that the woman religious has a new relationship with God's People: that of being a "mother for all."[18]

Part Three: The Language of Profession Rites

As African women religious articulate their experience in terms their own people can understand, the question of language becomes critically important; after all, an "insider view" of religious life is being expressed. There have already been significant attempts to re-formulate the consecration or vowing of African religious in local categories, attempts which go considerably beyond vernacular translations of imported formulae. Local religious try to come to terms with their experience of religious life and then find words in their mother

---

[18] Burke, *op. cit.*

tongue which can express for themselves and their people the meaning of that life. This reaching deep into the own lived experience, and wrapping words around the inner understanding, frees a person to give a new name to what may be called the "religious life movement" which initially came to Africa as an already inculturated institution, namely in a Western form. In the words of Arij Roest Crollius, "inculturation works itself out on the level of experience."[19] As with the Gospel itself, it is the inner meaning which needs to find an understandable local expression. Charles Kraft wrote, " ... the content expressed, not the forms in which that content was originally expressed, is sacred."[20] It is here that inculturation moves far beyond simple adaptation and accommodation. In Bosch's discussion of inculturation he argues that all theology is a particular discourse on a local experience of a universal message.[21] As a confirmation of this statement, a consideration of how African women religious themselves express their vow formulae – when they are free to do so in their own words and languages – reveals an evolving articulation of an African theology of religious life.

Below is a discussion of some of the language used by Nigerian women religious in vernacular vow formulae. It reflects how the experience of religious life is currently being expressed in local categories. Most of my information came from members of my own congregation which, since 1969, has a general policy of inviting members to write their own vow formulae: among the Sisters of Notre Dame de Namur, First Profession is commonly done in English, the language of formation; but for Final Profession the sisters are encouraged to express their formula of vows in their mother tongues. Each year, more and more of them accept this challenge. They do not find it easy, but they recognize that it is very rewarding and for the people unquestionably meaningful.

The Idea of Religious Consecration and the Vow

The basic local model on which the profession formula is based is that of a dedication or consecration of a person to the shrine of a local divinity. Usually, persons dedicate themselves to a shrine either because of a strong experience of being called (revealed in a dream, and confirmed by an oracle), or as a way

---

[19] Arij Roest Crollius, *What's So New about Inculturation?* (Inculturation: Working Papers on Living Faith and Cultures, 5, Rome: Gregorian University/Centre "Cultures et Religions", 1984), 15.

[20] In Norman Thomas (ed.), *Classic Texts in Mission and World Christianity: A Reader's Companion to David Bosch's Transforming Mission* (Maryknoll, NY: Orbis Books, 1995), 214; and, for a discussion of "dynamic equivalence theologies" see Charles Kraft, *Christianity in Culture* (Maryknoll, NY: Orbis Books, 1979), 291, 315, 318-319, 332.

[21] Bosch, *op. cit.*, 456-457.

to obtain protection in times of serious threat. These persons then come to be regarded as messengers of the divinity, and capable of serving for others as mediators with the divinity. Normally, such consecrated persons are clearly marked off by a sign, usually an indelible mark like a tattoo (but sometimes actually understood to be the external marker of an internal sign). This interesting idea has not yet produced any equivalent among religious (rings are used by some, but they are foreign).

Some people prefer to express the idea of making a vow with the word for *covenant*. This word is used among the *Igbo* by two people when they pledge themselves in marriage. It may also be used in the case of a blood pact between two persons. In both these instances, such a commitment is always understood to be irrevocable. Anyone who reneges on it will suffer serious consequences. In view of this, some local religious suggest that there might be some merit in the novice pronouncing her first, temporary vows, in English: this would avoid the embarrassment of using a vernacular word which can only be understood as being permanently binding.

The Expression of the Traditional Vows

Most women religious consider the actual wording of the vows problematic. For this reason, finding an appropriate local model for the ceremony is all the more important. Of the three traditional vows of religion, it is poverty and chastity that are particularly difficult to represent in local categories, for they are perceived as a veritable curse for the people.

Poverty: Any literal translation of this word to express the religious vow is meaningless since poverty never has any positive value for *Igbo* or *Afemai* people – or indeed for most Africans. Material poverty is considered a curse. Persons who are poor are judged to be so because they are lazy, or because they have not persevered in the struggle that life always is. Some sisters attempt to express the vow by ideas or images indicating *poverty of spirit*. But one *Afemai* sister used the expression "common ownership together" which has some resonance with the positive value placed on sharing in the traditional African setting. This was reflective of the sister's own understanding of the vow.

Chastity: Two attempts to express the sense of the vow of chastity drew directly on existing words, clumsily translatable as "not knowing man" (whether by not having sexual intercourse outside of marriage, denial of marriage itself, not indulging in flirting, or being sexually inactive like some married men and women). However, as with poverty, actually choosing to live in such a condition is generally seen as totally abnormal, since human beings have a duty to propagate their own or their partner's clan. One person went so far as to say, "A person who dies without issue has no chance of ever returning to the world through re-incarnation." But the *Igbo* word for this vow also means "to live a holy life." As we saw, persons dedicated to shrines and serving their people as mediators with a divinity are expected to live an irreproachable life. If their moral behavior is found lacking, this is a scandal and will be seriously censured.[22]

Yet another religious expressed her own understanding of the meaning of this vow: "living free in order to love all people without getting attached." This *Afemai* sister stressed that people do appreciate that religious live in a communal context. In contrast, the *Igbo* sisters remarked that their people would describe any person who was unmarried and without issue as "living alone" – which for them contradicts the very nature of human society.

Obedience: In both *Igbo* and *Afemai* social structure, obedience is a fundamental virtue and the hallmark of a respectable member of the society. Disobedient children are a source of great shame for their parents. Almost all the sisters simply adopted the word for obedience in their language, and used it to express the vow; they perceived a great correlation between its meaning in the social context and their own understanding of obedience in religious life. The exceptions were non-*Igbo* sisters. One modified the expression to emphasize the importance of listening, with allowance for self-expression and dialogue. Another preferred to use a phrase to express the vow: "listening to God through the voice of leaders." But for all, obedience in the socio-religious context always implies a junior-senior relationship, with the former bound to show respect and accept advice from their elders. In the case of age-mates, the word for obedience is used to express expected mutual respect and the keeping of secrets.

Conclusion

Historically, women religious were seen as unqualified to participate in the first evangelization of the African continent in the sixteenth and seventeenth centuries. Nevertheless, by the end of the nineteenth century they were considered by many of their male missionary counterparts as indispensable for the second evangelization. In today's church it seems women could become key agents of inculturation. Both their life among the people and their call to prayerfully reflect daily on their life experience make them eminently capable

---

[22] Mary J. Anochie, *The Igbo Woman and Consecrated Life* (Onitsha, Nigeria: Effective Key Publishers, 1994), 83ff.

of assuming a significant role in what Bediako has termed the "Africanization of the Christian experience."[23]

This presentation has examined some research-in-progress concerning how African women religious are slowly trying to articulate their understanding of their religious life. We have seen efforts to inculturate rituals of religious profession. Too often attention has only been given to the use of the African rhythm of music and dance, elements that risk becoming rather external or cosmetic. I have tried to identify the local models women religious draw on when they ritualize their profession of religious vows. More importantly, I have examined the degree to which they found ways to articulate, pronounce, utter and find words in their own languages for the meaning of religious life. It is evident that there is not yet a consensus on models; most of the rituals draw heavily on images taken from marriage, some modify a totally different context of meaning: that of dedication to the service of a traditional divinity. This in itself is a very interesting phenomenon; it indicates that religious are still searching for an appropriate way to celebrate and find words for the meaning of their lives. The challenge is not one of translation, but of trying to find words which communicate a lived understanding of meaning. It does seem to me that use of local languages – with local categories of thought and perception – is of central importance.

This study of profession rites has further implications. The material demonstrates that ministers and pastoral agents need to be sensitive to each faith community's need to *word* its own understanding of the Gospel and the received Christian tradition, both literally and figuratively, in speech and in performance. Until this is accomplished, inculturation is still in the air.

---

[23] Bediako, *op. cit.*, 4.

QUESTIONS

1. Here is another window onto inculturation. Reflecting on your own cultural experience and understanding of the Christian tradition, can you add to the material presented?

2. If people make up their own vows, is there not a danger of creating as much confusion as enlightenment, both in the religious community and the local church? What would you recommend, to minimize confusion or superficiality?

3. If each local church must inculturate the Gospel in its own way, is there a future for religious life as we know it? What advantages/disadvantages can you identify, in encouraging the kind of freedom advocated in this chapter?

4. Do you think religious communities of men would respond similarly to the women? What are the implications of your answer?

5. Can you identify signs of *organic progression* in this chapter (see Chapter One)? What other approaches to inculturation can you find?

LIST OF CONTRIBUTORS

IRENEO BARRETO, S.V.D., is a Paraguayan member of the Society of the Divine Word. Having worked among the *Tswana* people of Botswana, he successfully completed a Licentiate in Missiology from the Gregorian University in Rome. His contribution to this volume represents his first academic publication. It is taken from the research which he undertook in partial fulfilment of the requirements for his degree. Ireneo has a passion for integrating an understanding of cultures and languages with Christian faith and practice. He may be contacted via Kanamo Center, Box 143, Mahalapye, Botswana (Tel 00267-410491).

For almost twenty years, American Sister of Notre Dame de Namur *JOAN BURKE, S.N.D.-N.*, has been actively interested in the dynamics of inculturation in Africa. Trained as a social anthropologist (D.Phil., Oxford), her research – on the evolving African expression of African religious life – was undertaken over a period of eight years in the then Lower Zaire. Since 1991 she has been based in Nigeria. Until 1995 she served as Director for the Centre of Renewal in Jos, organizing leadership training seminars, spiritual development workshops, and retreats for men and women religious, clergy and laity. Since 1995 she has been a full-time member of the Provincial Leadership Team for her Congregation in Nigeria. She can be reached at Box 437, Auchi (Jattu), Edo State, Nigeria; and on-line at snduz@infoweb.abs.net.

Born in 1933 of Welsh and English parentage, *ADRIAN CAMPION EDWARDS, C.S.Sp.,* is a Cambridge graduate in social anthropology (Ph.D., 1959). After fieldwork among the *Ovimbundu* of Angola, he joined the Spiritans (Holy Ghost Fathers and Brothers) in England, was ordained in 1965, and went to Nigeria where he undertook an ethnographic study of the *Tiv* people. He accumulated seventeen years' experience in Nigeria and eight in Northern Cameroon, among several ethnic groups. With three years' (1970-1973) lecturing at the Missionary Institute, London, he has thus been parish priest, anthropologist, and professor – sometimes concurrently. Since 1996 he has taught anthropology and church history at the Séminaire Spiritain, Libreville, Gabon. Adrian is fascinated with hermeneutics and translation, and with the survival and transformation of cultures and languages. He dislikes suggestions that the missionary era is over, or that missionaries need not make strenuous efforts to learn local languages. (Address: Séminaire Spiritain, SP 3933, Libreville, Gabon)

The only contributor to this volume not based in Africa, *ANTHONY J. GITTINS, C.S.Sp.,* is currently the Bishop Francis X. Ford M.M. Professor of Missiology at the Catholic Theological Union in Chicago. English by birth, and trained in social anthropology at the University of Edinburgh (Ph.D., 1977), he worked in Sierra Leone among the *Mende* people from 1972 to 1980. Having subsequently taught at the Missionary Institute, London, for four years, he has been in Chicago since 1984. Ethnographic research and teaching have taken him to the *Maasai* people in Tanzania, the *Trobriand* Islanders and the *I-Kiribati* in the Pacific, as well as to other countries in Africa, to the Caribbean, and to Australia. A recent book is *Reading the Clouds: Mission Spirituality for New Times* (Liguori, 1999), and an ongoing project is ministry-and-research among the homeless population of Chicago. (Fax 773 728 9466; Email tgittins@ctu.edu)

Another Cambridge graduate in social anthropology is *JON KIRBY, S.V.D.* A Canadian citizen, he has worked in rural and urban ministries in Ghana since 1972. He is Founder and Director of the Tamale Institute of Cross-Cultural Studies (TICCS), a research and teaching institution of the Catholic church in Northern Ghana. TICCS offers field education and internship programs for Ghanaian priests, development workers, missionaries and other cross-cultural specialists in language-learning and applied cultural analysis for ministry and development. Jon's special interest is African traditional religion and problem-solving. (TICCS, Box 1012, Tamale, Ghana. Email TICCS@ug.gn.apc.org)

PIET KORSE, M.H.M., is a Dutch Mill Hill Missionary who has worked for twenty-six years in the Congo, where he directed a Research Centre for the study of *Mongo* culture. Having earned a Master's in spirituality from Loyola University, Chicago (1991), he returned as Director of a Cultural Research Centre among the *Basoga* people in Jinja, Uganda. His team studies the language and traditional religion. Diocesan Commissions attempt to incorporate the results of this research into the proclamation of the Gospel and the life of the church. His address is Cultural Research Centre, P. O. Box 1400, Jinja, Uganda (Tel 0043-21465).

The third member of the Society of the Divine Word represented in these pages is *KOFI RON LANGE, S.V.D.*, an American, who has worked in Ghana since 1968. An expert in local languages and fluent in three, he has researched and published extensively in the field designated "oral literature," and especially in Ghanaian proverbs. His particular interest lies in making connections between the oral wisdom of Ghana and that of Sacred Scripture. He is currently the Assistant Director of the Tamale Institute of Cross-Cultural Studies in Ghana. With Jon Kirby, he can be contacted at ticcs@africaonline.com.gh.

Born in Tanzania in 1946, *LAURENTI MAGESA* is a theologian, writer, and diocesan priest. He is recipient of the US Catholic Mission Association (USCMA) Award for his contributions to African Theology. At present he is engaged in pastoral ministry in Ingri-Bukama, Tanzania, as well as in research on aspects of African cultures and on the relationship between culture and Christianity. A recent book was *African Religion: The Moral Traditions of Abundant Life* (Orbis Books, 1997). (Address: Box 237, Tarime, Tanzania)

From the Belgian Province, and working in the Democratic Republic of Congo, *XAVIER PLISSART, M.Afr.*, writes poetically and harrowingly from Bukavu. Accompanying his article is an audio-tape containing some of the songs he mentions, as well as some photographs of the Archbishop whose assassination he chronicles. Further information on these can be obtained from tgittins@ctu.edu. There is also a pamphlet on the life and testimony of Archbishop Munzihirwa, which can be obtained from the Jesuit community in Kinshasa. (Fax contact in Brussels, Belgium: 0032 2 736 9713)

A diocesan priest of the Wa diocese in the Upper-Western Region of Ghana, *EDWARD B. TENGAN* was, until 1999, Professor of philosophy and anthropology at St. Victor's Major Seminary, Tamale, Ghana. He holds a Master's Degree in Religious Studies, a Licentiate in philosophy, and a Ph.D. in West African Studies. He is the author of *The Land as Being and Cosmos* [Sisala of N.W. Ghana], (Peter Lang, 1991); and *House of God: Church-as-Family from an African Experience* (Acco, 1997). He is currently parish priest of Ko parish in his home diocese, where he continues to engage in cultural research and the process of inculturation. (Address: Box 5, Nandom-Ko, Upper-West Region, Ghana)

STUDIA INSTITUTI MISSIOLOGICI SOCIETATIS VERBI DIVINI

1 Karl Müller (Hrsg.), *Missionsstudien*. VIII + 275 S. 1962. ISBN 3-87787-923-3; vergriffen

2 Louis J. Luzbetak, *The Church and Cultures. An Applied Missionary Anthropology*. XII + 417 S. 1963. ISBN 3-87787-924-1; vergriffen

3 Josef Schmitz, *Die Abra-Mission auf Nordluzon / Philippinen von 1598 bis 1955. Eine missionsgeschichtliche Untersuchung.* 216 S. 1964. ISBN 3-87787-018-X; vergriffen

4 Helenis Held, *Christendörfer. Untersuchung einer Missionsmethode*. XII + 96 S. 1963. ISBN 3-87787-019-8; vergriffen

5 Kurt Piskaty, *Die katholische Missionsschule in Nusa Tenggara (Südost-Indonesien)*. XXIV + 270 S. 1964. ISBN 3-87787-020-1; vergriffen

6 Fritz Bornemann, *Ein Briefwechsel zur Vorgeschichte von St. Ottilien*. 96 S. 1965. ISBN 3-87787-021-X

7 Paul Schebesta, *Portugals Konquistamission in Südost-Afrika*. XIV + 488 S. 1966. ISBN 3-87787-022-8

8 Fritz Bornemann, *Dr. Ludwig von Essen und seine Missionspläne*. 232 S. 1967. ISBN 3-87787-023-6

9 Horst Rzepkowski, *Thomas von Aquin und Japan. Versuch einer Begegnung*. 75 S. 1967. ISBN 3-87787-024-4; vergriffen

10 Paul Aoyama Gen, *Die Missionstätigkeit des heiligen Franz Xaver in Japan aus japanischer Sicht*. XVI + 182 S. 1967. ISBN 3-87787-025-2; vergriffen

11 Josef Kuhl, *Die Sendung Jesu und der Kirche nach dem Johannes-Evangelium*. XX + 242 S. 1967. ISBN 3-87787-026-2; vergriffen

12 Horst Rzepkowski, *Das Menschenbild bei Daisetz Teitaro Suzuki. Gedanken zur Anthropologie des Zen-Buddhismus*. XIII + 66 S. 1971. ISBN 3-87787-064-3; vergriffen

13 Horst Rzepkowski (Hrsg.), *Mission: Präsenz - Verkündigung - Bekehrung?* 168 S. 1974. ISBN 3-87787-066-X

14 Ewald Böning, *Der Pillánbegriff der Mapuche*. 203 S. 1974. ISBN 3-87787-084-8

15 Ortrud Stegmaier, *Der missionarische Einsatz der Schwestern auf den Inseln Flores und Timor (Südost-Indonesien)*. 118 S. 1974. ISBN 3-87787-075-9

16 Johannes Fleckner, *Thomas Kardinal Tien*. 138 S. 1975. ISBN 3-87787-080-5; vergriffen

17 Horst Baum, *Mut zum Schwachsein - in Christi Kraft. Grundelemente einer missionarischen Spiritualität nach dem zweiten Korintherbrief*. XXVI + 254 S. 1977. ISBN 3-87787-088-0; vergriffen

18 Rudolf Pöhl, *Der Missionar zwischen Ordensleben und missionarischemAuftrag*. 488 S.1977. ISBN 3-87787-095-3

19 António Martins da Torre, *A Igreja e a sua Tarefa Missionária segundo Emil Brunner*. 1977. XIX + 213 S. ISBN 3-87787-091-0

20 Sylwester Pajak, *Urreligion und Uroffenbarung bei P. W. Schmidt*. 235 S. 1978. ISBN 3-87787-081-3; vergriffen

21 Horst Rzepkowski (Hrsg.), *Allen alles werden*. 163 S. 1978. ISBN 3-87787-110-0

22 Sr. Regina Pacis Meyer, *Universales Heil, Kirche und Mission*. 232 S. 1979. ISBN 3-87787-111-9; vergriffen

23 Richard Hartwich, *P. Arnold Janssen und P. Josef Freinademetz. Briefwechsel 1904-1907*. 266 S. 1978. ISBN 3-87787-109-7

24 Karl Josef Rivinius, *Die katholische Mission in Süd-Shantung. Ein Bericht des Legationssekretärs Speck von Sternburg aus dem Jahre 1895 über die Steyler Mission in China*. 144 S. 1979. ISBN 3-87787-117-8

STUDIA INSTITUTI MISSIOLOGICI SOCIETATIS VERBI DIVINI

25 Wolfgang Hering, *Das Missionsverständnis in der ökumenisch-evangelikalen Auseinandersetzung*. 180 S. 1980. ISBN 3-87787-137-2

26 Richard Hartwich, *Johann Weig: Chronik der Steyler Mission in Tsingtao. 1923-1947*. 310 S. 1980. ISBN 3-87787-128-3

27 Augustine Kanjamala, *Religion and Modernization of India*. 371 S. 1981. ISBN 3-87787-138-0

28 Michael Coomans, *Evangelisatie en Kultuurverandering*. 340 S. 1980. ISBN 3-87787-140-2; vergriffen

29 Lawrence Nemer, *Anglican and Roman Catholic Attitudes on Missions*. 210 S. 1981. ISBN 3-87787-141-0; vergriffen

30 Joshua W. Sempebwa, *African Traditional Moral Norms and Their Implication for Christianity*. 271 S. 1983. ISBN 3-87787-165-8

31 Alain van der Beken, *Les Proverbes Yaka au Service de l'Annonce de l'Évangile*. 217 S. 1982. ISBN 3-87787-155-0

32 Richard Hartwich, *Steyler Missionare in China. I. Missionarische Erschließung Südshantungs (1879-1903)*. 582 S. 1983. ISBN 3-87787-166-6; vergriffen

33 Eugen Nunnenmacher, *Missionarisches Selbstverständnis nach dem Konzils-dekret „Ad Gentes" und nach persönlichen Außerungen von Afrikamissionaren*. XXXVI + 396 S. 1984. ISBN 3-87787-179-8

34 Karl Müller, *Friedrich Schwager (1876-1929). Pionier katholischer Missionswissenschaft*. 207 S. 1984. ISBN 3-87787-180-1

35 Antolin V. Uy, *The State of the Church in the Philippines 1850-1875. The Correspondence between the Bishops in the Philippines and the Nuncio in Madrid*. 266 S. 1984. ISBN 3-87787-181-X; vergriffen

36 Richard Hartwich, *Steyler Missionare in China. II. Bischof A. Henninghaus ruft Steyler Schwestern. 1904-1910. Beiträge zu einer Geschichte*. 626 S. 1985. ISBN 3-87787-189-5

37 Jacob Kavunkal, *To Gather Them into One. Evangelization in India Today - A Process of Building Community*. 225 S. 1985. ISBN 3-87787-198-4; vergriffen

38 Alain van der Beken, *L'Évangile en Afrique, vécu et commenté par des Bayaka*. 328 S. 1986. ISBN 3-87787-204-2; vergriffen

39 Karl Müller, *Mission Theology. An Introduction*. With Contributions by Hans-Werner Gensichen and Horst Rzepkowski. 237 S. 1987. ISBN 3-8050-0191-6

40 Richard Hartwich, *Steyler Missionare in China. III. Beiträge zu einer Geschichte: Republik China und Erster Weltkrieg 1911-1919*. 638 S. 1987. ISBN 3-8050-0180-0; vergriffen

41 Joachim G. Piepke (Hrsg.), *Anthropology and Mission. SVD International Consultation on Anthropology for Mission*. 127 S. 1988. ISBN 3-8050-0217-3

42 Richard Hartwich, *Steyler Missionare in China. IV. Geistlicher Führer seiner Chinamissionare Rev.mus P. Wilh. Gier SVD, 1922 - Beiträge zu einer Geschichte*. 110 S. 1988. ISBN 3-8050-0202-5; vergriffen

43 Josef Alt (Hrsg.), *Arnold Janssen SVD, Briefe nach Südamerika. Bd I. 1890-1899*. 448 S. 1989. ISBN 3-8050-0231-9

44 Josef Alt (Hrsg.), *Arnold Janssen SVD, Briefe nach Südamerika. Bd II. 1900-1902*. 531 S. 1991. ISBN 3-8050-0267-X

45 Josef Alt (Hrsg.), *Arnold Janssen SVD, Briefe nach Südamerika. Bd III. 1903-1904*. 514 S. 1992. ISBN 3-8050-0292-0

46 Josef Alt (Hrsg.), *Arnold Janssen SVD, Briefe nach Südamerika. Bd IV. 1905-1908*. 533 S. 1993. ISBN 3-8050-0323-4

STUDIA INSTITUTI MISSIOLOGICI SOCIETATIS VERBI DIVINI

47 Karl Müller, *Josef Schmidlin (1876-1944). Papsthistoriker und Begründer der katholischen Missionswissenschaft.* 441 S. 1989. ISBN 3-8050-0246-7

48 Richard Hartwich (Hrsg.), *Steyler Missionare in China. V. Aus Kriegsruinen zu neuen Grenzen. 1920-1923.* 528 S. 1989. ISBN 3-8050-0242-4

49 Johannes A. Bauer, *Das Presseapostolat Arnold Janssens (1837-1909). Seine Bedeutung für die Entfaltung der Gesellschaft des Göttlichen Wortes und die Ausbildung des Missionsbewußtseins.* 100 S. 1989. ISBN 3-8050-0254-8

50 Angela Feder, *Reinkarnationshypothese in der New Age-Bewegung.* 101 S. 1991. ISBN 3-8050-0281-5

51 Theo Sundermeier/Volker Küster (Hrsg.), *Das schöne Evangelium. Christliche Kunst im balinesischen Kontext.* 99 S. 1991. ISBN 3-8050-0285-8

52 Yoshifumi Torisu, *Gott und Welt. Eine Untersuchung zur Gotteslehre des Irenäus von Lyon.* 268 S. 1991. ISBN 3-8050-0286-6

53 Richard Hartwich, *Steyler Missionare in China. VI. Auf den Wogen des Bürgerkrieges. 1924-1926.* 675 S. 1991. ISBN 3-8050-0288-2

54 J. Huppertz, *Ein Beispiel katholischer Verlagsarbeit in China. Eine zeitgeschichtliche Studie.* 167 S. 1992. ISBN 3-8050-0304-8

55 Juan Bockwinkel, *Steyler Indianermission in Paraguay 1910-1925.* 179 S. 1992. ISBN 3-8050-0305-6

56 Kurt Piskaty/Horst Rzepkowski (Hrsg.), *Verbi Praecones. Festschrift für P. Karl Müller SVD zum 75. Geburtstag.* 397 S. 1993. ISBN 3-8050-0324-2

57 Josef Alt (Hrsg.), *Arnold Janssen SVD, Briefe in die Vereinigen Staaten von Amerika.* 494 S. + 16 Bildseiten. 1994. ISBN 3-8050-0339-0

58 Josef Alt (Hrsg.), *Arnold Janssen SVD, Leters to the United States of America.* English Edition Translated by Robert Pung, SVD, and Peter Spring. 552 S. 1998. ISBN 3-8050-0405-2

59 Edmund Woga, *Der parentale Gott. Zum Dialog zwischen der Religion der indonesischen Völker Sumbas und dem Christentum.* 439 S. 1994. ISBN 3-8050-0344-7

60 Martin Üffing, *Die deutsche Kirche und Mission. Konsequenzen aus dem nachkonziliaren Missionsverständnis für die deutsche Kirche.* 285 S. 1994. ISBN 3-8050-0346-3

61 Paul Steffen, *Missionsbeginn in Neuguinea. Die Anfänge der Rheinischen, Neuendettelsauer und Steyler Missionsarbeit in Neuguinea.* 316 S. 1995. ISBN 3-8050-0351-X

62 Volker Küster, *Theologie im Kontext. Zugleich ein Versuch über die Minjung-Theologie.* 192 S. 1995. ISBN 3-8050-0362-5

63 Josef Alt (Hrsg.), *Arnold Janssen SVD. Briefe nach Neuguinea und Australien.* LVI + 451 S. + 20 Bildseiten. 1996. ISBN 3-8050-0370-6

64 Karl Müller, *Kontemplation und Mission. Steyler Anbetungsschwestern 1896-1996.* XII + 532 S. + Bilddokumentation. 1996. ISBN 3-8050-0374-9

65 Stephen Bevans, SVD/Roger Schroeder, SVD (eds.), *Word Remembered, Word Proclaimed. Selected Papers from Symposia Celebrating the SVD Centennial in North America.* 255 S. 1997. ISBN 3-8050-0398-6

66 Maria Dlugosz SSpS, *Mae Enga Myths and Christ's Message. Fullness of Life in Mae Enga Mythology and Christ the Life (Jn 10:10).* 302 S. + 6 Karten. 1998. ISBN 3-8050-0403-6

67 Ursula Kubera, *Frauen in der Missionierung Sambias.* 537 S. 1998. ISBN 3-8050-0410-9

68 Roberto Francisco Daniel, *Befreiungstheologie im Film. Eine Analyse des Films „Deus e o Diabo na Terra do Sol" von Glauber Rocha.* 137 S. 1998. ISBN 3-8050-0416-8

69 Karl Müller, *Contemplation and Mission. Sister-Servants of the Holy Spirit of Perpetual Adoration.* Translated by Frank Mansfield SVD, 448 S. 1998. ISBN 3-8050-0419-2

Neuerscheinungen - Recently published:

70 Josef Alt SVD, *Arnold Janssen. Lebensweg und Lebenswerk des Steyler Ordensgründers,* 1085 S. 1999. ISBN 3-8050-0427-3

71 Ludger Anton Müller SVD, *Die Geschichte der Indianermission der Steyler Missionare in Paraguay (1910-1925).* 211 S. 1999. ISBN 3-8050-0437-0

Steyler Verlag, Bahnhofstraße 9, D-41334 Nettetal, Germany
Tel: [0049] (02157) 12 02 24; Fax: [0049] (02157) 12 02 22